LIGHT & EASY
Italian
COOKING

CONTENTS

EDITORIAL
Food Editor Sheryle Eastwood
Assistant Food Editor Rachel Blackmore
Home Economist Anneka Mitchell
Recipe Development Jane Ash, Susan Bell,
Carolyn Feinberg, Joanne Glynn,
Michelle Gorry, Donna Hay
Food Consultant Frances Naldrett
Text Denise Greig, Alison Magney
Editorial Co-ordinator Margaret Kelly
Subeditor Ella Martin

STYLING
Michelle Gorry

PHOTOGRAPHY
Harm Mol

ILLUSTRATIONS
Carol Dunn

PRODUCTION
Margie Mulray
Chris Hatcher

COVER DESIGN
Frank Pithers

DESIGN AND PRODUCTION
MANAGER
Nadia Sbisa

PUBLISHER
Philippa Sandall

Published by J.B. Fairfax Press Pty Ltd
80-82 McLachlan Avenue
Rushcutters Bay NSW Australia 2011

LIGHT AND EASY ITALIAN COOKING
Includes Index
ISBN 1 86343 019 9

Formatted by J.B. Fairfax Press Pty Ltd
Output by Adtype, Sydney
Printed by Toppan Printing Co, Hong Kong

Distributed in Australia by
Newsagents Direct Distributors
150 Bourke Road, Alexandria NSW

Distributed Internationally by
T.B. Clarke (Overseas) Pty Ltd
80 McLachlan Avenue
Rushcutters Bay NSW 2011
Tel: (02) 360 7566 Fax: (02) 360 7445

Distributed in UK by
J.B. Fairfax Press Ltd
9 Trinity Centre, Park Farm Estate
Wellingborough, Northants
Ph: (0933) 402330 Fax: (0933) 402234

NZ agents Medialine Holdings Ltd
P O Box 100 243
North Shore Mail Centre
Tel: (09) 443 0250 Fax: (09) 443 0249

CHECK-AND-GO

Use the easy Check-and-Go boxes which appear beside each ingredient. Simply check your pantry and if the ingredients are not there, tick the boxes as a reminder to add those items to your shopping list.

CANNED FOODS

Can sizes vary between countries and manufacturers. You may find the quantities in this book are slightly different to what is available. Purchase and use the can size nearest to the suggested size in the recipe.

SOUPS
and
STARTERS

Nothing is more appetising than an antipasto table brimming with delicious choices, unless there's also a bubbling tureen of soup to start the meal! The choice is yours.

EASY ANTIPASTO PLATTER FOR SIX

An antipasto platter is fun as a starter for an Italian meal, or is great to serve when friends drop by.

- ❖ **Vegetable Toss**
- ❖ **Crostini**
- ❖ **Prosciutto with Melon Wedges**
- ❖ **Creamy Tuna Spread**
- ❖ **Salami Platter**
- ❖ **Marinated Olives**
- ❖ **Spicy Eggplant (Aubergine) with Dipping Sauce (recipe page 6)**

VEGETABLE TOSS

Make this dish several hours ahead of time to allow the flavours to develop.

Serves 6

- ☐ **2 tablespoons olive oil**
- ☐ **4 zucchini (courgettes), cut into slices, lengthways**
- ☐ **1 large head broccoli, cut into florets**
- ☐ **2 carrots, peeled**

DRESSING
- ☐ **2 small red chillies, finely chopped**
- ☐ **1 tablespoon finely chopped fresh mint**
- ☐ **1 tablespoon finely chopped fresh oregano**
- ☐ **125 mL (4 fl oz) light olive oil**
- ☐ **2 tablespoons red wine vinegar**
- ☐ **2 tablespoons lemon juice**
- ☐ **freshly ground black pepper**

1   Heat oil in a frypan and cook zucchini (courgettes) slices until golden on each side. Drain on absorbent kitchen paper and set aside.

2   Boil, steam or microwave broccoli until tender. Refresh under cold water. Drain and set aside.

3   Slice carrots into long thin strips, using a vegetable peeler. Boil, steam or microwave until just tender. Refresh under cold water. Drain and set aside.

4   To make dressing, place chillies, mint, oregano, oil, vinegar and lemon juice in a screw-top jar. Season to taste with pepper. Shake well to combine. Place vegetables in a serving bowl and toss through dressing. Cover and refrigerate until required.

CROSTINI

This recipe can be made using any of your favourite breads.

Serves 6

- ☐ **1 Italian bread stick, cut into 1 cm (¹/₂ in) slices**
- ☐ **90 g (3 oz) butter, melted**

1   Brush both sides of bread slices lightly with butter and place on an oven tray.

2   Bake at 180°C (350°F/Gas 4) for 12 minutes, or until golden and crunchy.

CREAMY TUNA SPREAD

This spread is great served with Crostini or fresh crusty bread.

Serves 6

- ☐ 185 g (6 oz) canned tuna, drained
- ☐ 125 g (4 oz) cream cheese
- ☐ 125 g (4 oz) mayonnaise
- ☐ 2 tablespoons lemon juice
- ☐ 125 g (4 oz) butter, melted
- ☐ 1 teaspoon snipped fresh chives
- ☐ 1 teaspoon chopped fresh thyme

Place tuna, cream cheese, mayonnaise and lemon juice in a food processor or blender and process until smooth. With machine running, add butter, chives and thyme. Transfer mixture to a serving dish and refrigerate for 1 hour or until firm.

SALAMI SELECTION

Serves 6

- ☐ 125 g (4 oz) each of any 2 types of Italian salami, sliced. A few of these include alesandre, felino, cotto, felinetti, calabrese, Napoli, Milano and Genoa
- ☐ 125 g (4 oz) each of any 2 types of Italian hams or sausages, sliced. Choose from pastrami, pancetta, mortadella and pepperoni

Cut or fold salami, hams and sausages to make your platter look appealing.

MARINATED OLIVES

These olives will keep for up to four months in the refrigerator.

Makes 1 medium (600 mL/1 pt) jar

- ☐ 375 g (12 oz) olives

MARINADE

- ☐ 125 mL (4 fl oz) light olive oil
- ☐ 60 mL (2 fl oz) balsamic vinegar
- ☐ 1 tablespoon chopped fresh tarragon
- ☐ 2 bay leaves
- ☐ 2 tablespoons chopped fresh basil
- ☐ 2 teaspoons freshly ground black pepper

Place olives in a large sterilised jar. Mix together oil, vinegar, tarragon, bay leaves, basil and black pepper. Pour over olives to cover. Seal jar and store in refrigerator.

PROSCIUTTO WITH MELON WEDGES

Serves 6

- ☐ 1 cantaloupe or honeydew melon, halved, seeded and peeled
- ☐ 16 slices prosciutto ham

Cut melon into long thin wedges, wrap a slice of prosciutto around each wedge of melon and secure with a toothpick. Arrange on platter and chill before serving.

Clockwise from top: Vegetable Toss, Creamy Tuna Spread, Spicy Eggplant (Aubergine) with Dipping Sauce (page 6), Marinated Olives, Salami Selection, Crostini, Prosciutto with Melon Wedges

Platter Jenny Orchard Background Porters Lime Wash

ANCHOVY AND TOMATO RICE BALLS

Serves 6

- ☐ **185 g (6 oz) plain flour**
- ☐ **1 egg, lightly beaten with 1 tablespoon milk**
- ☐ **125 g (4 oz) dried breadcrumbs**
- ☐ **vegetable oil for cooking**
- ☐ **60 g (2 oz) butter, melted**
- ☐ **2 cloves garlic, crushed**
- ☐ **freshly ground black pepper**
- ☐ **1 eggplant (aubergine), cut into 6 thick slices**

RICE BALLS

- ☐ **250 g (8 oz) short-grain rice, cooked**
- ☐ **125 g (4 oz) ricotta cheese**
- ☐ **30 g (1 oz) grated fresh Parmesan cheese**
- ☐ **2 eggs, lightly beaten**
- ☐ **1 tablespoon finely chopped fresh parsley**

FILLING

- ☐ **60 g (2 oz) grated mozzarella cheese**
- ☐ **8 anchovy fillets, drained and chopped**
- ☐ **30 g (1 oz) sun-dried tomatoes, drained and chopped**

SAUCE

- ☐ **2 teaspoons oil**
- ☐ **1 onion, finely chopped**
- ☐ **1 clove garlic, crushed**
- ☐ **440 g (14 oz) canned tomato puree (passata)**
- ☐ **2 tablespoons red wine**
- ☐ **¹/₂ teaspoon sugar**
- ☐ **freshly ground black pepper**

1   To make rice balls, place rice, ricotta cheese, Parmesan cheese, eggs and parsley in a bowl and mix well. Divide mixture into six even portions and set aside.

2   To make filling, place mozzarella, anchovies and sun-dried tomatoes in a bowl and mix well. Shape into six balls and mould a portion of rice mixture around each ball. Roll balls in flour, dip in egg mixture, then roll in breadcrumbs. Refrigerate for 30 minutes.

3   Combine butter, garlic and black pepper to taste. Brush both sides of eggplant (aubergine) slices with butter mixture. Place on an oven tray and bake at 180°C (350°F/Gas 4) for 20 minutes.

SPICY EGGPLANT (AUBERGINE) WITH DIPPING SAUCE

Serves 6

- ☐ **1 eggplant (aubergine), cut in half lengthways, then into 5 mm (¹/₄ in) slices**
- ☐ **salt**
- ☐ **185 g (6 oz) cornflour**
- ☐ **vegetable oil for cooking**

DIPPING SAUCE

- ☐ **1 red pepper, seeded and roughly chopped**
- ☐ **100 mL (3¹/₂ fl oz) cream (single)**
- ☐ **75 g (2¹/₂ oz) butter, chopped**
- ☐ **¹/₄ teaspoon chilli powder**
- ☐ **freshly ground black pepper**

BATTER

- ☐ **125 g (4 oz) self-raising flour, sifted**
- ☐ **200 mL (6¹/₂ fl oz) milk**
- ☐ **2 eggs, lightly beaten**

1   Sprinkle eggplant (aubergine) slices with salt and set aside for 30 minutes.

2   To make sauce, place red pepper and cream in a food processor or blender and process until smooth. Transfer to a small saucepan and cook over a low heat for 5 minutes. Remove from heat and whisk in butter. Season to taste with chilli and black pepper. Set aside and keep warm.

3   To make batter, sift flour into a small bowl, make a well in the centre and gradually stir in milk and eggs. Mix to form a smooth paste. Set aside.

4   Rinse eggplant (aubergine) well under cold running water. Drain and pat dry on absorbent kitchen paper. Toss eggplant (aubergine) in cornflour and shake to remove excess.

5   Heat oil in a frypan. Dip eggplant (aubergine) slices in batter, and cook a few at a time until golden brown. Drain on absorbent kitchen paper. Serve eggplant (aubergine) with warm sauce.

4   To make sauce, heat oil in a small saucepan and cook onion and garlic for 5 minutes or until transparent. Stir in tomato puree, wine and sugar, and cook over a low heat, stirring occasionally, for 10 minutes. Season to taste with pepper and set aside to keep warm.

5   Heat oil in a frypan and cook rice balls over a medium heat until golden. To serve, divide sauce between six plates. Place an eggplant (aubergine) slice in the centre of each plate then top with a rice ball.

COOK'S TIP

When making the rice balls, you will find it easier if you dampen your hands before rolling the rice balls in flour.

❖

BACON AND SALAMI-WRAPPED FENNEL

Serves 6

- [ ] **2 fennel bulbs**
- [ ] **90 g (3 oz) butter, softened**
- [ ] **¹/₂ teaspoon caraway seeds, ground**
- [ ] **1 teaspoon ground cumin**
- [ ] **12 slices salami**
- [ ] **12 bacon rashers, trimmed**

SAUCE
- [ ] **2 teaspoons oil**
- [ ] **2 cloves garlic, crushed**
- [ ] **375 mL (12 fl oz) beef stock**
- [ ] **125 mL (4 fl oz) red wine**
- [ ] **2 teaspoons cornflour, blended with 1 tablespoon water**

1   To make sauce, heat oil in a small saucepan and cook garlic for 3-4 minutes or until golden. Pour in stock and wine and cook over a low heat for 25 minutes. Stir in cornflour mixture and cook stirring constantly, for 2-3 minutes or until sauce thickens. Set aside and keep warm.

2   Remove base of fennel bulb, separate leaves and trim each piece. Boil, steam or microwave fennel pieces until soft. Set aside to cool. Combine butter, caraway seeds and cumin. Spread inside of each piece of fennel with butter mixture, top with a slice of salami, then roll up and wrap with a bacon rasher. Secure with a toothpick. Grill for 3-4 minutes or until bacon is crisp. Spoon sauce over rolls.

Cheesy Walnut Flans (page 8),
Roasted Pepper Salad, Bacon and Salami-
Wrapped Fennel

❖

ROASTED PEPPER SALAD

The sweetness of the peppers mixed with a tangy vinaigrette makes a wonderful starter or part of an antipasto platter. Make at least an hour before serving to allow the flavour to develop.

Serves 6

- [ ] **2 red peppers, halved and seeded**
- [ ] **2 yellow or green peppers, halved and seeded**
- [ ] **500 g (1 lb) spinach, stalks removed and leaves finely shredded**
- [ ] **125 g (4 oz) button mushrooms**
- [ ] **155 g (5 oz) pitted black olives**

VINAIGRETTE
- [ ] **125 mL (4 fl oz) light olive oil**
- [ ] **60 mL (2 fl oz) balsamic vinegar**
- [ ] **2 teaspoons chopped fresh basil**
- [ ] **1 teaspoon chopped fresh marjoram**
- [ ] **freshly ground black pepper**

1   Place red and yellow peppers skin side up under a preheated grill and cook until skins are black and charred. Place in a plastic food bag, seal and set aside for 5 minutes to make peeling easier. Remove peppers from bag, peel away skins and wash well under cold water. Cut into strips and set aside to cool.

2   Arrange spinach on a platter, top with peppers, mushrooms and olives.

3   To make vinaigrette, place oil, vinegar, basil and marjoram in a screw-top jar. Season to taste with black pepper. Shake well to combine. Pour over salad.

Salad Bowl G & C Ventura Plates and Salad Servers Made Where

CHEESY WALNUT FLANS

Serves 6

PASTRY
- [ ] **155 g (5 oz) butter**
- [ ] **1 tablespoon vegetable oil**
- [ ] **185 g (6 oz) Gorgonzola cheese, crumbled**
- [ ] **2 egg yolks**
- [ ] **2 tablespoons water**
- [ ] **250 g (8 oz) plain flour, sifted**

FILLING
- [ ] **125 g (4 oz) chopped walnuts, lightly toasted**
- [ ] **375 g (12 oz) ricotta cheese**
- [ ] **30 g (1 oz) grated Parmesan cheese**
- [ ] **3 eggs, lightly beaten**
- [ ] **185 mL (6 fl oz) milk**
- [ ] **1/2 teaspoon ground (grated) nutmeg**
- [ ] **1/2 teaspoon freshly ground black pepper**
- [ ] **1 tablespoon snipped fresh chives**

1   To make pastry, place butter and oil in a bowl and mix until soft and creamy. Stir in Gorgonzola cheese, egg yolks and water, and mix to combine. Add flour and mix until a soft firm dough forms. Roll dough into a ball. Wrap in plastic food wrap and refrigerate for 30 minutes.

2   To make filling, place walnuts, ricotta cheese, Parmesan cheese, eggs, milk, nutmeg, black pepper and chives in a bowl, and mix to combine.

3   Roll out pastry between two layers of greaseproof paper and cut to fit six well-greased 12 cm (5 in) flan tins. Line pastry flans with baking paper and fill with dried beans or rice. Bake at 180°C (350°F/Gas 4) for 8 minutes. Remove beans and paper and bake for 5 minutes longer.

4   Spoon filling into pastry cases and cook for 15 minutes or until filling is firm.

COUNTRY CHICKEN AND PASTA SOUP

Serves 6

- [ ] **3 litres (5 1/4 pt) chicken stock**
- [ ] **4 chicken breast fillets, skinned**
- [ ] **1 teaspoon whole black peppercorns**
- [ ] **4 bay leaves**
- [ ] **1 sprig fresh rosemary**
- [ ] **1 onion, chopped**
- [ ] **1 red pepper, seeded and chopped**
- [ ] **2 carrots, chopped**
- [ ] **250 g (8 oz) cabbage, shredded**
- [ ] **185 g (6 oz) short pasta shapes, such as macaroni**
- [ ] **2 tablespoons grated Parmesan cheese**

1   Place stock in a large saucepan and bring to the boil. Add chicken breasts, peppercorns, bay leaves and rosemary. Reduce heat, cover and simmer for 20 minutes or until chicken is cooked.

2   Remove chicken from pan and set aside. Strain stock and return to cleaned saucepan. Stir in onion, red pepper, carrots, cabbage and pasta. Cover and simmer for 20 minutes, or until pasta is cooked.

3   Slice chicken, stir into soup and cook for 5 minutes longer. Just prior to serving, stir Parmesan cheese through.

MINTED EGGPLANT (AUBERGINE) SOUP

This soup can be served hot or cold.

Serves 6

- [ ] **1 tablespoon vegetable oil**
- [ ] **2 onions, finely chopped**
- [ ] **3 eggplants (aubergines), peeled and diced**
- [ ] **500 mL (16 fl oz) chicken stock**
- [ ] **250 mL (8 fl oz) water**
- [ ] **freshly ground black pepper**
- [ ] **250 mL (8 fl oz) cream (single)**
- [ ] **2 tablespoons chopped fresh mint**

1   Heat oil in a large saucepan and cook onions for 5 minutes or until golden. Add eggplant (aubergine) and cook for 5 minutes longer. Stir in stock, water and black pepper to taste. Reduce heat and simmer for 35 minutes.

2   Remove from heat, transfer to a food processor or blender and process until smooth. With machine running, add cream and mint and process until combined.

---

3   To serve soup hot, place in a clean saucepan and heat soup gently until simmering. To serve soup cold, place in a bowl, cover and chill for at least 2 hours.

CHILLED BRANDY FIG AND APPLE SOUP

Serves 4

- [ ] **4 dried figs, sliced**
- [ ] **60 mL (2 fl oz) brandy**
- [ ] **30 g (1 oz) butter**
- [ ] **1 tablespoon brown sugar**
- [ ] **4 cooking apples, peeled, cored and thinly sliced**
- [ ] **1/4 teaspoon ground ginger**
- [ ] **125 mL (4 fl oz) apple juice**
- [ ] **250 mL (8 fl oz) water**
- [ ] **250 mL (8 fl oz) thickened cream (double)**

Serviette Ring and Stainless Steel Bowl Vasa Agencies Floor Ware Collingwood Floors

1   Place figs in a bowl, pour brandy over and set aside for 30 minutes.

2   Melt butter in a large saucepan. Add sugar and stir over a medium heat until sugar dissolves. Add figs, brandy, apples and ginger and cook for 5 minutes.

3   Stir in apple juice, and water. Cover and cook over a low heat for 12 minutes. Remove from heat and cool slightly. Then transfer to a food processor or blender and process until smooth. With machine running, pour in cream and process until combined. Transfer soup into a large bowl, cover and refrigerate for at least 4 hours before serving.

Hearty Bean and Tomato Soup, Chilled Brandy Fig and Apple Soup, Minted Eggplant (Aubergine) Soup, Country Chicken and Pasta Soup

❖

HEARTY BEAN AND TOMATO SOUP

Serve this delicious soup as a main meal or for lazy Sunday lunches.

Serves 6

- [ ]   **250 g (8 oz) bacon rashers, chopped**
- [ ]   **1 onion, finely chopped**
- [ ]   **2 cloves garlic, crushed**
- [ ]   **1 kg (2 lb) tomatoes, peeled, seeds removed and chopped**
- [ ]   **125 g (4 oz) concentrated tomato paste**
- [ ]   **1 litre (1³/₄ pt) vegetable stock or water**
- [ ]   **125 g (4 oz) cannellini or white haricot beans, soaked overnight and drained**
- [ ]   **125 g (4 oz) chick peas, soaked overnight and drained**
- [ ]   **125 g (4 oz) borlotti beans, soaked overnight and drained**
- [ ]   **3 tablespoons chopped fresh parsley**
- [ ]   **1 tablespoon chopped fresh oregano or 1 teaspoon dried oregano**

1   Place bacon in a large saucepan and cook over a medium heat for 3-4 minutes, or until fat starts to melt. Add onion and garlic and cook for 5-6 minutes, or until onion is transparent.

2   Stir in tomatoes, tomato paste, stock, cannellini beans, chick peas and borlotti beans. Bring to the boil, cover, reduce heat and simmer for 2 hours, or until beans are tender. Just prior to serving, stir parsley and oregano through.

GOOD FOOD
from
THE SEA

Italy is surrounded on most sides by sea, and you'll be surrounded on all sides by people clamouring for more of these tasty, easy Italian seafood dishes.

❖
OCTOPUS IN RED WINE MARINADE

This easy dish takes a little time to cook but it looks after itself and is absolutely delicious. The octopus almost caramelises as it cooks, and melts in your mouth as you eat it.

Serves 4

- [ ] **500 g (1 lb) baby octopus, cleaned**

MARINADE
- [ ] **60 mL (2 fl oz) olive oil**
- [ ] **500 mL (16 fl oz) red wine**
- [ ] **1 clove garlic, crushed**
- [ ] **1 teaspoon sugar**

1   To make the marinade, combine oil, wine, garlic and sugar in a bowl. Add octopus and set aside to marinate for 1 hour.
2   Transfer octopus and marinade to a saucepan. Simmer for 1-1¹/₂ hours or until octopus is tender.

❖
SARDINE FRITTERS

Sardines are abundant in Italian waters. This recipe can be prepared several hours before cooking. Serve as an entree, or increase quantities and serve with salad and bread for a main meal.

Serves 4

- [ ] **12 fresh sardines, scaled**
- [ ] **4 tablespoons plain flour**
- [ ] **1 egg, blended with 2 tablespoons milk**

- [ ] **125 g (4 oz) dried breadcrumbs**
- [ ] **oil for cooking**

MINTED CHILLI BUTTER
- [ ] **125 g (4 oz) butter, softened**
- [ ] **3 tablespoons finely chopped fresh mint**
- [ ] **2 spring onions (shallots), finely chopped**
- [ ] **1 clove garlic, crushed**
- [ ] **¹/₄ teaspoon chopped red chilli**
- [ ] **freshly ground black pepper**

1   Cut heads from sardines and using scissors cut along the underside of the fish. Clean and open out flat. Cut backbone at tail end and gently remove. Wash sardines and dry on absorbent kitchen paper.
2   Coat sardines in flour, dip in egg mixture, then coat with breadcrumbs.
3   To make Minted Chilli Butter, place butter, mint, spring onions (shallots), garlic and chilli in a bowl and mix well. Place butter on a piece of plastic food wrap and roll into a log shape. Refrigerate until required.
4   Heat oil and one-third Minted Chilli Butter in a large frypan and cook sardines for 1-2 minutes each side or until golden. Serve sardines topped with a slice of Minted Chilli Butter.

Sardine Fritters, Octopus in Red Wine Marinade, Mediterranean Fish Stew

MEDITERRANEAN FISH STEW

Serves 6

- ☐ **10 green-lipped mussels, scrubbed and beards removed**
- ☐ **250 g (8 oz) uncooked prawns**
- ☐ **750 g (1½ lb) fish fillets (such as bream, red snapper or mullet), cut into large pieces**
- ☐ **250 g (8 oz) calamari rings**

SAUCE

- ☐ **1 tablespoon olive oil**
- ☐ **2 leeks, finely sliced**
- ☐ **2 cloves garlic, crushed**
- ☐ **125 mL (4 fl oz) dry white wine**
- ☐ **1 large red pepper, finely chopped**
- ☐ **440 g (14 oz) canned Italian peeled tomatoes, undrained and mashed**
- ☐ **125 mL (4 fl oz) chicken stock**
- ☐ **1 teaspoon grated lemon rind**
- ☐ **1 bay leaf**
- ☐ **pinch cayenne pepper**
- ☐ **3 tablespoons chopped fresh parsley**
- ☐ **freshly ground black pepper**

1 To make sauce, heat oil in a large saucepan. Cook leeks and garlic for 3-4 minutes or until tender. Stir in wine, and cook over a high heat until wine is nearly evaporated. Mix in pepper, tomatoes, stock, lemon rind, bay leaf and cayenne pepper. Bring to the boil.

2 Add mussels to pan and cook until shells open. Remove from pan and set aside. Discard any mussels that do not open. Stir in prawns, fish and calamari and cook for 2-3 minutes. Return mussels to the pan and stir in parsley. Season to taste with black pepper and serve immediately.

TOMATOES

Tomatoes are now so much a part of Italian cooking it is hard to imagine it without them. They are, however, a fairly recent addition to Italian cooking. It was not until the sixteenth century that they were brought to Europe from Mexico and Peru. The tomato was first known as pomme d'amour or 'love apple'. Over time the name changed to pomme d'or or 'golden apple' and even today the Italian name for tomato is pomodoro.

❖

TUNA IN PIQUANT TOMATO SAUCE

Serves 4

- ☐ **1 tablespoon olive oil**
- ☐ **4 fresh tuna cutlets**

SAUCE
- ☐ **1 onion, chopped**
- ☐ **2 cloves garlic, crushed**
- ☐ **440 g (14 oz) canned Italian peeled tomatoes, undrained and mashed**
- ☐ **125 mL (4 fl oz) tomato juice**
- ☐ **2 tablespoons capers, chopped**
- ☐ **4 anchovy fillets, chopped**
- ☐ **¹/₂ teaspoon dried oregano**
- ☐ **freshly ground black pepper**

1   Heat oil in a frypan and cook tuna for 2-3 minutes each side. Transfer to an ovenproof dish and reserve juices.
2   To make sauce, cook onion and garlic in pan for 4-5 minutes or until tender. Add reserved pan juices, tomatoes, tomato juice, capers, anchovies and oregano. Season to taste with black pepper. Bring to the boil and pour over tuna. Cover and bake at 180°C (350°F/Gas 4) for 20-30 minutes, or until tuna flakes when tested.

❖

SPICY SCALLOPS AND MUSHROOMS

Scallops, mushrooms and garlic are a wonderful combination in this quick dish.

Serves 4

- ☐ **45 g (1¹/₂ oz) butter**
- ☐ **500 g (1 lb) button mushrooms**
- ☐ **6 spring onions (shallots), chopped**
- ☐ **2 cloves garlic, crushed**
- ☐ **500 g (1 lb) scallops, cleaned**
- ☐ **60 mL (2 fl oz) dry white wine**
- ☐ **1 red chilli, seeded and finely sliced**
- ☐ **3 tablespoons chopped fresh parsley**

1   Melt butter in a large frypan and cook mushrooms, spring onions (shallots) and garlic for 4-5 minutes. Remove from pan and set aside. Add scallops to pan and cook for 2-3 minutes or until tender. Remove from pan and set aside.
2   Stir in wine, chilli and parsley and cook over a high heat until reduced by half. Return mushroom mixture and scallops to pan, toss to combine.

Tuna in Piquant Tomato Sauce, Spicy Scallops and Mushrooms

GARLIC TIPS

✧   To crush garlic, peel and chop the required number of cloves, sprinkle with salt and crush with the broad side of a large knife.

✧   For a milder garlic flavour do not crush the garlic, simply add the unpeeled clove during cooking and remove it before serving.

✧   To remove the smell of garlic from a wooden chopping board, rub the surface with lemon juice. This also works well to remove onion odours from chopping boards.

✧   As garlic dries and ages its flavour becomes sharper and less is required.

CHEESY STUFFED SQUID

Serves 4

- [ ] **4 small squid hoods, cleaned**
- [ ] **2 tablespoons olive oil**
- [ ] **1 clove garlic, crushed**
- [ ] **440 g (14 oz) canned Italian peeled tomatoes, undrained and mashed**
- [ ] **$^{1}/_{2}$ teaspoon dried rosemary**
- [ ] **60 mL (2 fl oz) dry white wine**
- [ ] **$^{1}/_{2}$ teaspoon sugar**
- [ ] **freshly ground black pepper**

STUFFING
- [ ] **45 g (1$^{1}/_{2}$ oz) breadcrumbs, made from stale bread**
- [ ] **4 tablespoons chopped fresh parsley**
- [ ] **125 g (4 oz) ricotta cheese**
- [ ] **3 tablespoons grated fresh Parmesan cheese**
- [ ] **$^{1}/_{2}$ teaspoon dried oregano**
- [ ] **1 clove garlic, crushed**
- [ ] **pinch cayenne pepper**
- [ ] **1 egg, lightly beaten**

1 To make stuffing, combine breadcrumbs, parsley, ricotta cheese, Parmesan cheese, oregano, garlic, cayenne and egg. Divide mixture into four equal portions and spoon into squid hoods. Secure ends with a toothpick or skewer.
2 Heat oil in a frypan and cook squid for 3-4 minutes each side or until brown. Add garlic, tomatoes, rosemary, wine, sugar and black pepper to taste. Reduce heat and simmer for 20-30 minutes or until squid is tender. To serve, remove skewers, slice squid and accompany with sauce.

❖

LEMONY PRAWN KEBABS

These are delightful on the barbecue.

Serves 4

- [ ] **750 g (1$^{1}/_{2}$ lb) uncooked large prawns, peeled and deveined**
- [ ] **16 button mushrooms, stalks removed**
- [ ] **2 green peppers, seeded and cut into 16 pieces**

MARINADE
- [ ] **60 mL (2 fl oz) olive oil**
- [ ] **2 tablespoons lemon juice**
- [ ] **2 cloves garlic, crushed**
- [ ] **1 small red chilli, seeded and finely chopped**
- [ ] **1 tablespoon chopped fresh sage**
- [ ] **freshly ground black pepper**

1 To make marinade, place oil, lemon juice, garlic, chilli and sage in a bowl. Season to taste with black pepper and mix to combine. Add prawns and mushrooms and toss to coat with marinade. Set aside to marinate for 1 hour.
2 Thread prawns, mushrooms and green peppers alternately onto eight oiled wooden skewers. Grill kebabs for 8-10 minutes or until cooked, turning and basting with marinade during cooking.

COOK'S TIP

When using wooden skewers, do not forget to soak them in cold water for at least an hour before using under the grill or on the barbecue. This will prevent them from burning.

Lemony Prawn Kebabs, Cheesy Stuffed Squid

TROUT WRAPPED IN PROSCIUTTO

Serves 4

- ☐ **4 medium trout (280 g/9 oz each), scaled and cleaned**
- ☐ **1 tablespoon olive oil**
- ☐ **8 long slices prosciutto**
- ☐ **4 sprigs fresh thyme (optional)**

MARINADE
- ☐ **5 tablespoons olive oil**
- ☐ **3 tablespoons lemon juice**
- ☐ **2 cloves garlic, crushed**
- ☐ **1 tablespoon chopped fresh thyme or 1 teaspoon dried thyme**
- ☐ **freshly ground black pepper**

1　To make marinade, combine oil, lemon juice, garlic and thyme. Season to taste with black pepper. Place trout in a shallow dish and pour marinade over. Cover and refrigerate for 2 hours.

2　Cut four pieces of baking paper large enough to enclose each trout. Brush each sheet of paper with oil. Place 2 slices prosciutto side by side on each sheet of paper. Remove trout from marinade and place on prosciutto. Place a sprig of thyme in the cavity of each trout and wrap prosciutto around trout. Pour remaining marinade over. Fold baking paper around trout to enclose. Seal edges by rolling together tightly.

3　Place parcels on an oven tray and bake at 180°C (350°F/Gas 4) for 20-25 minutes, or until trout flakes when tested.

❖

GARLIC AND ROSEMARY MACKEREL CUTLETS

Serves 4

- ☐ **1 tablespoon olive oil**
- ☐ **30 g (1 oz) butter**
- ☐ **2 cloves garlic, crushed**
- ☐ **4 large mackerel cutlets or thick fillets**
- ☐ **3 tablespoons lemon juice**
- ☐ **2 teaspoons fresh rosemary leaves, or ¹/₂ teaspoon dry rosemary leaves**
- ☐ **freshly ground black pepper**

1　Heat oil and butter in a large frypan and cook garlic for 1 minute. Add cutlets, and cook for 3-4 minutes each side or until browned.

2　Pour lemon juice over and sprinkle with rosemary. Season to taste with black pepper. Cover and simmer for 5-8 minutes or until flesh flakes when tested with a fork.

WHOLE FISH WITH LEEK AND RICE SEASONING

Serves 4

- ☐ **4 whole small fish (such as snapper or bream), cleaned and scored**
- ☐ **125 mL (4 fl oz) dry white wine**
- ☐ **60 g (2 oz) butter, melted**

STUFFING
- ☐ **2 tablespoons olive oil**
- ☐ **2 leeks, sliced**
- ☐ **2 cloves garlic, crushed**
- ☐ **185 g (6 oz) long-grain rice, cooked**
- ☐ **3 tablespoons pine nuts**
- ☐ **4 tablespoons sultanas**
- ☐ **1 stalk celery, chopped**
- ☐ **3 tablespoons chopped fresh parsley**
- ☐ **1 teaspoon lemon pepper**

1 To make stuffing, heat oil in a frypan. Cook leeks and garlic for 3-4 minutes or until tender. Remove from heat and stir in rice, pine nuts, sultanas, celery, parsley and lemon pepper.

2 Fill cavity of each fish with stuffing, close cavity and secure with a skewer. Place fish in a single layer in a greased shallow baking dish. Pour wine and butter over and bake at 180°C (350°F/Gas 4) for 35-45 minutes, or until fish flesh flakes when tested with a fork. Baste 3-4 times during cooking, adding more wine if necessary. Place fish on serving plates, cover and keep warm. Pour pan juices into a small saucepan. Boil to reduce, remove from heat and pour over fish. Serve immediately.

MICROWAVE IT

✧ Whole fish cooks well in the microwave – the eyes should be removed before cooking as they can explode.

✧ Whole fish is best cooked on a MEDIUM-HIGH (70%) power setting, allowing 5-6 minutes per 500 g (1 lb) of fish.

Garlic and Rosemary Mackerel Cutlets, Whole Fish with Leek and Rice Seasoning, Trout Wrapped in Prosciutto

Wall Ware Collingwood Floors *Salt and Pepper Shakers* Vasa Agencies *Column* Pazotti *Marble Plates* Villeroy & Boch

RICE, GNOCCHI
and
POLENTA

Few things are more delicious than a creamy risotto, a dish of feather-light gnocchi, or freshly baked polenta. The best results require a little patience, but they are worth every minute.

❖

POLENTA, CHEESE AND PROSCIUTTO LOAF

This loaf makes an attractive and filling light meal.

Serves 6

- ☐ **200 g (6¹/₂ oz) very thinly sliced prosciutto**
- ☐ **1.8 litres (3 pt) water**
- ☐ **200 g (6¹/₂ oz) polenta**
- ☐ **2 teaspoons snipped fresh chives**
- ☐ **2 teaspoons chopped fresh parsley**
- ☐ **2 teaspoons chopped fresh mint**
- ☐ **30 g (1 oz) butter, cut into pieces**
- ☐ **freshly ground black pepper**
- ☐ **1 egg white, lightly beaten**
- ☐ **155 g (5 oz) grated fontina cheese**

1   Line a lightly oiled 23 x 12 cm (9 x 5 in) loaf dish with prosciutto, leaving 2 cm (³/₄ in) to overhang top.
2   Bring water to the boil in a large saucepan. Reduce heat and gradually whisk in polenta, cook over a low heat stirring frequently for 40 minutes, or until mixture forms a mass and pulls away from side of pan. Stir chives, parsley, mint and butter through polenta. Season to taste with black pepper.
3   Brush prosciutto with egg white. Spoon half polenta mixture into the dish, pressing out evenly. Top with fontina cheese leaving 5 mm (¹/₄ in) around edges free of cheese. Cover with remaining polenta mixture. Press down firmly to give a smooth mould. Fold over prosciutto to encase loaf. Bake at 180°C (350°F/Gas 4) for 15-20 minutes. Allow to stand 15-20 minutes before slicing.

❖

SPINACH, GREEN PEA AND RICOTTA GNOCCHI

Serves 4

- ☐ **220 g (7 oz) fresh spinach leaves, or 200 g (6¹/₂ oz) frozen spinach, thawed and drained**
- ☐ **220 g (7 oz) shelled fresh or frozen green peas**
- ☐ **220 g (7 oz) ricotta cheese, drained**
- ☐ **freshly ground black pepper**
- ☐ **ground (grated) nutmeg**
- ☐ **60 g (2 oz) butter**
- ☐ **2 eggs, lightly beaten**
- ☐ **90 g (3 oz) grated fresh Parmesan cheese**
- ☐ **3 tablespoons dried breadcrumbs**
- ☐ **5 tablespoons plain flour**

1   Steam or microwave spinach until tender. Drain and squeeze to remove excess liquid. Set aside.
2   Boil, steam or microwave peas until tender. Drain and combine with spinach. Chop mixture finely.
3   Place ricotta and spinach mixture in a saucepan. Season to taste with black pepper and nutmeg. Add 15 g (¹/₂ oz) butter and cook over a very low heat, stirring frequently until butter melts and all excess liquid evaporates. Remove from heat. Beat in eggs, then half the Parmesan cheese, breadcrumbs and flour. The mixture should be firm enough to hold its shape, but soft enough to give a light-textured gnocchi.
4   Using well-floured hands, take heaped tablespoons of mixture and roll lightly into small ovals. Bring a large saucepan of water to the boil, then reduce heat. Drop in a few at a time and cook for 4·5 minutes or until they rise to the surface. Remove from pan and drain. Cover and keep warm.
5   Melt remaining butter in a saucepan and cook until lightly browned. Pour butter over gnocchi, sprinkle with remaining Parmesan cheese and serve.

❖

RISOTTO WITH PARMESAN CHEESE

Serves 4

- ☐ **1.2 litre (2 pt) chicken or beef stock**
- ☐ **45 g (1¹/₂ oz) butter**
- ☐ **2 tablespoons vegetable oil**
- ☐ **1 small onion, finely chopped**
- ☐ **315 g (10 oz) Arborio rice**
- ☐ **60 g (2 oz) grated fresh Parmesan cheese**
- ☐ **freshly ground black pepper**

1   Place stock in a large saucepan and bring to the boil. Reduce heat and simmer.
2   Melt 30 g (1 oz) butter and oil in a separate saucepan and cook onion over a low heat for 5-6 minutes or until lightly golden. Add rice and stir for 1-2 minutes. This will coat the grains well with the butter mixture. Pour in 200 mL (6¹/₂ oz) boiling stock and stir over a medium heat until liquid is absorbed.
3   Continue cooking in this way until stock is used and rice is just tender; this will take 18-20 minutes. Stir frequently during cooking to prevent sticking.
4   Stir Parmesan cheese through with remaining butter. Season to taste with black pepper and serve immediately.

Variations

Risotto with Asparagus and Bacon: Make up Risotto with Parmesan Cheese cooking 2 bacon rashers, chopped with the onion. Cook 500 g (1 lb) fresh asparagus in boiling stock. When tender, remove and set aside to cool, then cut into 5 cm (2 in) pieces. Fold through risotto just prior to serving.
Risotto with Spinach and Herbs: Make up Risotto with Parmesan Cheese cooking 2 crushed cloves garlic with the onion. Cook 440 g (14 oz) spinach until tender, drain and chop finely. Fold spinach with 1 tablespoon finely chopped fresh basil and 1 tablespoon finely chopped fresh oregano through cooked risotto.

Risotto with Parmesan Cheese, Polenta, Cheese and Prosciutto Loaf, Spinach, Green Pea and Ricotta Gnocchi

❖

RICE WITH MOZZARELLA AND HERBS

Much simpler than a risotto, this dish relies on the quality of the fresh herbs and mozzarella used.

Serves 4

- ☐ 4 litres (7 pt) water
- ☐ 315 g (10 oz) Arborio rice
- ☐ 90 g (3 oz) butter, cut into small pieces
- ☐ 2 tablespoons chopped mixed fresh herbs
- ☐ 250 g (8 oz) grated mozzarella cheese
- ☐ 60 g (2 oz) grated fresh Parmesan cheese
- ☐ freshly ground black pepper

1   Place water in a large saucepan and bring to the boil. Add rice and cook, covered, for 15-20 minutes or until the rice is just tender. Stir occasionally during cooking to prevent sticking.

2   Drain, then return rice to same pan. Stir butter and chopped herbs through. Fold mozzarella and Parmesan cheeses through and season to taste with black pepper. Transfer to a warm serving dish and serve immediately.

❖

BAKED POLENTA WITH SALAMI AND TOMATOES

When polenta is presented as a pie and baked it is known as Polenta Pasticciata. There are many different versions – probably as many as there are housewives in northern Italy. This one is easy and sure to draw compliments when served.

Serves 4

- ☐ 1 litre (1³/₄ pt) water
- ☐ 220 g (7 oz) polenta
- ☐ 90 g (3 oz) butter, cut into pieces
- ☐ 300 g (9¹/₂ oz) mushrooms, sliced
- ☐ freshly ground black pepper
- ☐ 2 x 440 g (14 oz) canned Italian tomatoes, drained, seeds squeezed out and chopped
- ☐ 175 g (5¹/₂ oz) Italian salami, thinly sliced
- ☐ 60 g (2 oz) grated fresh Parmesan cheese

SAUCE

- ☐ 45 g (1¹/₂ oz) butter
- ☐ 1 small bay leaf
- ☐ 3 tablespoons plain flour
- ☐ 500 mL (16 fl oz) milk
- ☐ freshly ground black pepper
- ☐ pinch ground (grated) nutmeg

1   To make sauce, melt butter in a small saucepan, add bay leaf and stir in flour. Cook over a medium heat for 1 minute. Remove from heat and gradually blend in milk. Season to taste with black pepper and nutmeg. Cook over a medium heat, stirring constantly until sauce boils and thickens. Set aside.

2   Place water in a large saucepan and bring to the boil. Gradually whisk in polenta. Reduce heat and cook for 20 minutes, stirring frequently.

3   Melt half the butter in a frypan and cook mushrooms over a low heat for 2-3 minutes. Season to taste with black pepper.

4   Remove polenta from heat and stir remaining butter through. Spread one-third polenta into a greased ovenproof dish. Top with one-third mushrooms, one-third tomatoes, one-third salami and one-third sauce. Repeat these layers twice, ending with a final layer of sauce. Sprinkle with Parmesan cheese and bake at 200°C (400°F/Gas 6) for 30 minutes. Stand for 5-10 minutes before serving.

Rice with Mozzarella and Herbs, Baked Polenta with Salami and Tomatoes

❖

GNOCCHI ALLA ROMANA

This baked gnocchi, made with semolina, is quite versatile and can be served as a course on its own, as an accompaniment to a main meal, or as a base for vegetables.

Serves 4

- ☐ **1 litre (1³/₄ pt) milk**
- ☐ **3 egg yolks, lightly beaten**
- ☐ **250 g (8 oz) semolina flour**
- ☐ **90 g (3 oz) butter, cut into pieces**
- ☐ **ground (grated) nutmeg**
- ☐ **freshly ground black pepper**
- ☐ **90 g (3 oz) grated fresh Parmesan cheese**

1   Place milk in a large, heavy-based saucepan and bring to just below boiling point. Mix 2-3 tablespoons hot milk with egg yolks and set aside.

2   Gradually stir semolina into hot milk. Add half the butter and season to taste with nutmeg and black pepper. Cook over a medium heat, stirring constantly, until mixture becomes very thick.

3   Remove from heat and stir in 30 g (1 oz) Parmesan cheese. Gradually stir in egg mixture, then beat until smooth. Transfer to a large shallow dish and spread out to 1 cm (¹/₂ in) thick. Set aside to cool.

4   Cut gnocchi into circles using a 4 cm (1¹/₂ in) cutter and layer, slightly overlapping, in a greased, shallow ovenproof dish. Melt remaining butter and drizzle over gnocchi. Sprinkle with remaining Parmesan cheese and bake at 200°C (400°F/Gas 6) for 15 minutes or until golden.

POLENTA

Polenta is, simply, cooked yellow maize flour (farina gialla or grano-turco in Italian), but there is nothing simple about its significance to the cooks of northern Italy. Its uses are infinite, and it can turn up on the table in many guises. It can be eaten alone with butter and Parmesan, or shaped into fingers and fried in oil and garlic, or baked in the oven to serve with roasts. Cold polenta is cut into slices and eaten as bread in some areas.

Fabrics Potpourri Column Lifestyle Imports Bowl Private Life

Gnocchi Alla Romana

PRESERVED *is* BETTER

'Fresh is Best' the saying goes, but Italians regularly prove that 'Preserved is Better'. A fresh tomato is one thing; a sun-dried tomato coated with a light oil is quite another. See how cleverly you can transform the mundane ...

SICILIAN PRESERVED EGGPLANT (AUBERGINE)

Serve preserved eggplant (aubergine) as part of an antipasto selection, or as a vegetable accompaniment to cooked meats.

Makes 1 large (1 litre/1³/₄ pt) jar

- ☐ **1 kg (2 lb) baby eggplant (aubergine), cut lengthways into thin strips**
- ☐ **3 tablespoons salt**
- ☐ **2 tablespoons finely chopped fresh mint**
- ☐ **3 cloves garlic, crushed**
- ☐ **1 teaspoon finely chopped fresh oregano**

- ☐ **2 tablespoons red wine vinegar**
- ☐ **3 small red chillies, seeded and sliced**
- ☐ **410 mL (13 fl oz) extra virgin olive oil**

1   Sprinkle eggplant (aubergine) slices with salt and set aside to stand for 2 hours. Rinse and pat dry.
2   Combine eggplant (aubergine), mint, garlic, oregano and 1 tablespoon vinegar. Layer eggplant (aubergine) and chillies in a warm sterilised jar. Press down firmly and add remaining vinegar and enough olive oil to cover. Seal and refrigerate until required.

Sicilian Preserved Eggplant (Aubergine), Bocconcini Marinated with Herbs, Roasted Peppers in Olive Oil, Spiced Olives

❖

BOCCONCINI MARINATED WITH HERBS

Serve bocconcini sliced with assorted salad leaves and a little of the marinade spooned over.

Serves 8

- ☐ **500 g (1 lb) fresh bocconcini, drained and dried**
- ☐ **3 cloves garlic, peeled**
- ☐ **2 sprigs fresh oregano**
- ☐ **2 sprigs fresh thyme**
- ☐ **1 sprig fresh parsley**
- ☐ **1 bay leaf**
- ☐ **3 small red chillies**
- ☐ **200 mL (6½ fl oz) extra virgin olive oil**

Place bocconcini, garlic, oregano, thyme, parsley, bay leaf and chillies in a sterilised jar. Cover with olive oil. Seal jar and refrigerate for up to 2 weeks.

❖

ROASTED PEPPERS IN OLIVE OIL

Roasting peppers gives them a succulent, sweet taste. This can be done over coals, a gas flame or under the grill.

Makes 1 medium (600 mL/1 pt) jar

- ☐ **4 red peppers, roasted until black**
- ☐ **4 yellow peppers, roasted until black**
- ☐ **2 teaspoons salt**
- ☐ **3 cloves garlic, peeled**
- ☐ **200 mL (6½ fl oz) extra virgin olive oil**

1   Cut peppers in half, remove seeds and skin. Slice into large pieces.
2   Sprinkle peppers with salt and pack into a warm sterilised jar. Add garlic cloves and cover with oil. Allow to settle, cover and refrigerate until required.

❖

SPICED OLIVES

Serve these olives as part of an antipasto platter, to top pizzas, or in salads for an extra special flavour.

Makes 1 medium (600 mL/1 pt) jar

- ☐ **500 g (1 lb) Kalamata olives**
- ☐ **2 cloves garlic, chopped**
- ☐ **3 small red chillies, chopped**
- ☐ **2 tablespoons chopped fresh parsley**
- ☐ **3 bay leaves**
- ☐ **200 mL (6½ fl oz) extra virgin olive oil**

Combine olives, garlic, chillies and parsley. Place olive mixture and bay leaves in a warm sterilised jar. Cover with olive oil, seal and refrigerate until required.

Tiles Pazotti Floor Ware Collingwood Floors

BOCCONCINI

Bocconcini are small balls of fresh mozzarella cheese. If they are unavailable you can use fresh mozzarella cut into cubes instead.

MARINATED MUSHROOMS

Use small fresh button mushrooms for this recipe. If larger mushrooms are used you will find that it is best to slice them to allow flavours to permeate.

Makes 1 jar (750 mL/1¼ pt)

- ☐ 1 lemon
- ☐ 500 g (1 lb) small button mushrooms, wiped over and stems trimmed
- ☐ 250 mL (8 fl oz) water
- ☐ 5 cloves garlic, peeled
- ☐ 1 teaspoon whole black peppercorns
- ☐ 3 sprigs fresh thyme
- ☐ 3 bay leaves
- ☐ 2 tablespoons white wine vinegar
- ☐ 1 teaspoon salt
- ☐ 300 mL (9½ fl oz) extra virgin olive oil

1   Cut strips of lemon rind from lemon and set aside. Squeeze juice of lemon over the mushrooms.
2   Place lemon rind, water, garlic, peppercorns, thyme, bay leaves, vinegar and salt in a small saucepan. Simmer, uncovered, for 10 minutes, then bring to the boil. Add mushrooms and cook for 2 minutes. Strain mushrooms and reserve thyme and bay leaves. Pack mushrooms, lemon rind, thyme and bay leaves into sterilised jars.
3   Cover with oil, seal and store in a dark cupboard for 5 days. Transfer and store in refrigerator until required. Bring mushrooms to room temperature before serving.

SUN-DRIED TOMATOES

Traditionally, tomatoes are dried on racks in the sun. This can be achieved successfully only if weather conditions and time permits. This method, using a low temperature in a conventional oven, gives good results.

Makes 1 small (125 mL/4 fl oz) jar

- ☐ 12 plum tomatoes, washed and halved
- ☐ 200 mL (6½ fl oz) extra virgin olive oil

1   Place tomatoes in single layer on oven tray. Cook for 12 hours at 110°C (225°F/Gas ¼), turning occasionally until dry.
2   Remove from oven and set aside to cool. Pack into warm sterilised jars and pour oil over. Refrigerate until required.

BOLOGNESE PICKLED ONIONS

These onions can be eaten and enjoyed within 48 hours of making, but they are best if left for a month until they are fully pickled and have become an appealing purple colour.

- ☐ 1 litre (1¾ pt) water
- ☐ 2 tablespoons salt
- ☐ 1 teaspoon sugar
- ☐ 15 small white onions, peeled
- ☐ 1 bay leaf
- ☐ 600 mL (1 pt) red wine vinegar

1   Place water, salt and sugar in a saucepan and bring to the boil. Add onions and cook for 1 minute. Drain and pat dry with absorbent kitchen paper. Set aside to cool completely.
2   Place onions and bay leaf in a warm sterilised jar. Cover with vinegar and seal. Store in a dark place for 1 month.

CHICK PEAS IN GARLIC OIL

Serve chick peas as an appetiser at room temperature, or warm. They also make an interesting addition to an antipasto platter.

Makes 1 medium (500 mL/16 fl oz) jar

- ☐ 185 g (6 oz) dried chick peas
- ☐ 300 mL (9½ fl oz) extra virgin olive oil
- ☐ 4 cloves garlic, crushed
- ☐ freshly ground black pepper
- ☐ 3 tablespoons lemon juice
- ☐ 3 tablespoons chopped fresh parsley

1   Place chick peas in a small saucepan and cover with cold water. Bring to the boil, then turn off heat, cover and soak for 1 hour. Drain and cover with fresh cold water. Cover pan and cook over a low heat for 2-3 hours or until tender. Drain well.
2   Heat oil in a frypan and cook garlic and chick peas until lightly browned. Season to taste with black pepper and mix in lemon juice and parsley. Pack into a warm sterilised jar, seal and refrigerate until required.

Marinated Mushrooms, Sun-Dried Tomatoes, Bolognese Pickled Onions, Chick Peas in Garlic Oil

Column John Normyle *Table* Private Life *Fabric* Potpourri

PASTA
and
SAUCES

Pasta comes in all shapes and sizes. When you see these sauce ideas and baked pasta dishes, you'll understand why the Italians love it so. Viva Pasta!

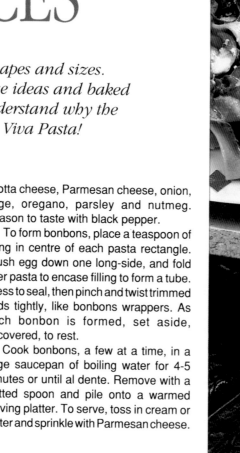

❖

BONBONS FILLED WITH CHICKEN AND HERBS

These look wonderful when made with different coloured pastas. If served as an entree this recipe will serve six.

Serves 4

BONBONS
- [ ] **6 sheets fresh plain, tomato or spinach flavoured pasta (27 x 24 cm/11 x 9¹/₂ in)**
- [ ] **1 egg, lightly beaten**
- [ ] **cream (single) or melted butter for coating**
- [ ] **grated fresh Parmesan cheese**

FILLING
- [ ] **200 g (6¹/₂ oz) cooked chicken meat, finely diced**
- [ ] **60 g (2 oz) ham, finely diced**
- [ ] **155 g (5 oz) ricotta cheese, drained**
- [ ] **2 tablespoons grated fresh Parmesan cheese**
- [ ] **¹/₂ onion, grated**
- [ ] **¹/₂ teaspoon finely chopped fresh sage**
- [ ] **¹/₂ teaspoon finely chopped fresh oregano**
- [ ] **¹/₂ teaspoon finely chopped fresh parsley**
- [ ] **pinch ground (grated) nutmeg**
- [ ] **ground black pepper**

1 Cut each pasta sheet into nine rectangles 8 x 9 cm (3 x 3¹/₂ in). Trim shorter ends of each rectangle using a zigzag pastry wheel. Set pasta aside and cover with a damp cloth.

2 To make filling, combine chicken, ham,

ricotta cheese, Parmesan cheese, onion, sage, oregano, parsley and nutmeg. Season to taste with black pepper.

3 To form bonbons, place a teaspoon of filling in centre of each pasta rectangle. Brush egg down one long-side, and fold over pasta to encase filling to form a tube. Press to seal, then pinch and twist trimmed ends tightly, like bonbons wrappers. As each bonbon is formed, set aside, uncovered, to rest.

4 Cook bonbons, a few at a time, in a large saucepan of boiling water for 4-5 minutes or until al dente. Remove with a slotted spoon and pile onto a warmed serving platter. To serve, toss in cream or butter and sprinkle with Parmesan cheese.

COOK'S TIP

✧ These bonbons are best made with homemade pasta rolled thinly.

✧ For something different you might like to make parcels rather than bonbons. To make parcels, cut 5 cm (2 in) circles of pasta and place teaspoon of filling in centre of each circle then gather up edges to form a pouch and pinch together to seal. Cook and serve as described in the recipe above.

Open Mushroom Ravioli, Bonbons filled with Chicken and Herbs, Tagliatelle with Spinach and Mushrooms (page 26)

Fabrics Potpourri Column John Normyle Wooden Bowl Private Life

❖

OPEN MUSHROOM RAVIOLI

A stylish approach for a wonderful entree. A delicious filling is visible between the unjoined sides of pasta.

Serves 4

- [ ] **16 circles plain or tomato fresh pasta, 4-5 cm (1½-2 in) in diameter, or refer Homemade Pasta, (page 36)**
- [ ] **4 dried porcini or cepes**
- [ ] **90 mL (3 fl oz) hot water**
- [ ] **90 g (3 oz) butter**
- [ ] **220 g (7 oz) button mushrooms, thinly sliced**
- [ ] **3 tablespoons white port or dry sherry**
- [ ] **3 tablespoons cream (single)**
- [ ] **1½ tablespoons chicken stock**
- [ ] **pinch ground (grated) nutmeg**
- [ ] **freshly ground black pepper**
- [ ] **1 small bunch watercress**
- [ ] **4 tablespoons thick sour cream**

1   Cook pasta circles, a few at a time, in boiling water in a large saucepan for 4-5 minutes or until tender. Remove and lay out in a single layer to dry, on clean tea-towels.

2   Place porcini and hot water in a bowl and set aside to soak for 30 minutes. Drain porcini and chop finely. Reserve liquid.

3   Melt 30 g (1 oz) butter in a frypan and gently cook fresh mushrooms for 2-3 minutes. Stir in soaked porcini and reserved liquid. Blend in port, cream, stock and nutmeg. Season to taste with black pepper. Cook over a medium heat until mixture reduces and thickens. Stir in remaining butter.

4   Place 2 pasta circles on each serving plate. Top each circle with 1-2 tablespoons mushroom mixture, then a few sprigs of watercress. Partially cover with another circle of pasta. Top each ravioli with a dollop of sour cream and garnish with watercress. Serve immediately.

TAGLIATELLE WITH SPINACH AND MUSHROOMS

Serves 4

- ☐ 500 g (1 lb) fresh tomato tagliatelle, or 410 g (13 oz) dried tomato tagliatelle
- ☐ 60 g (2 oz) butter
- ☐ 1 clove garlic, crushed
- ☐ 2 tablespoons Marsala
- ☐ 250 g (8 oz) button mushrooms, sliced
- ☐ 250 mL (8 fl oz) thickened cream (double)
- ☐ freshly ground black pepper
- ☐ 750 g (1½ lb) fresh spinach, stalks removed and leaves shredded
- ☐ grated fresh Parmesan cheese

1 Cook tagliatelle in boiling water in a large saucepan until al dente. Drain, set aside and keep warm.
2 Melt butter in a saucepan and cook garlic and Marsala over a low heat for 3 minutes or until syrupy. Add mushrooms and cook for 3 minutes longer. Blend in cream and bring to the boil. Season to taste with black pepper.
3 Add pasta to sauce. Toss in spinach and stir to coat. Cook over a low heat for 2-3 minutes, or until spinach is warmed through. Serve with Parmesan cheese.

THREE-CHEESE SAUCE WITH PISTACHIOS

Serves 4

- ☐ 250 mL (8 fl oz) cream (single)
- ☐ 90 g (3 oz) Gorgonzola, crumbled
- ☐ 75 g (2½ oz) grated fresh Parmesan cheese
- ☐ 60 g (2 oz) grated fresh romano or Parmesan cheese
- ☐ 60 g (2 oz) shelled pistachio nuts, chopped
- ☐ 1 teaspoon finely chopped fresh basil
- ☐ ground white pepper

Place cream in a saucepan and bring to the boil. Reduce heat, add Gorgonzola cheese and stir until melted and smooth. Stir in Parmesan and romano cheeses. Cook over a low heat, stirring constantly until sauce is thick and smooth. Add pistachio nuts and basil. Season to taste with white pepper. To serve, spoon sauce over cooked pasta of your choice.

RICOTTA AND HERB SAUCE

Serves 4

- ☐ 1 egg yolk
- ☐ 155 g (5 oz) ricotta cheese
- ☐ 90 mL (3 fl oz) thickened cream (double)
- ☐ 4 tablespoons grated fresh Parmesan cheese
- ☐ 1 teaspoon finely snipped fresh chives
- ☐ 1 teaspoon finely chopped fresh parsley
- ☐ coarsely ground white pepper

Three-Cheese Sauce with Pistachios, Ricotta and Herb Sauce, Mussel, Tomato and Orange Sauce, Anchovy and Green Olive Sauce

1 Beat egg yolk into ricotta cheese and mix until smooth. Set aside.

2 Heat cream in a saucepan, stir in Parmesan cheese, chives and parsley. Season to taste with white pepper. Beat through ricotta mixture just before serving. Spoon sauce over cooked pasta.

❖

MUSSEL, TOMATO AND ORANGE SAUCE

Serves 4

- ☐ **3 x 440 g (14 oz) canned Italian peeled tomatoes, drained**
- ☐ **$1^1/_2$ tablespoons olive oil**
- ☐ **1 onion, chopped**
- ☐ **1 clove garlic, crushed**
- ☐ **$^1/_2$ teaspoon dried chilli flakes**
- ☐ **200 mL ($6^1/_2$ fl oz) dry white wine**
- ☐ **3 teaspoons finely chopped fresh oregano, or 1 teaspoon dried**
- ☐ **$^1/_2$ teaspoon sugar**
- ☐ **3 tablespoons orange juice**
- ☐ **freshly ground black pepper**
- ☐ **16 mussels, cleaned and scrubbed**
- ☐ **2 teaspoons grated orange rind**
- ☐ **2 tablespoons finely chopped fresh parsley**

1 Squeeze tomatoes to push out seeds, pulping flesh as you go.

2 Heat oil in a large saucepan and cook onion, garlic and chilli flakes for 5 minutes. Mix in tomatoes, 100 mL ($3^1/_2$ fl oz) wine, oregano, sugar and orange juice. Season to taste with pepper. Bring to the boil, then reduce heat and simmer for 40 minutes, or until sauce reduces and thickens.

3 Place mussels in a baking dish and pour in remaining white wine. Bake at 220°C (425°F/Gas 7) for 8-10 minutes or until mussels open. Discard any unopened mussels.

4 Combine orange rind and parsley. Toss mussels into sauce and sprinkle with parsley mixture.

❖

ANCHOVY AND GREEN OLIVE SAUCE

Serves 4

- ☐ **155 g (5 oz) pitted green olives, sliced**
- ☐ **1 teaspoon finely chopped anchovy fillets**
- ☐ **60 g (2 oz) grated fresh Parmesan cheese**
- ☐ **60 g (2 oz) walnuts, finely chopped**
- ☐ **2 teaspoons chopped fresh oregano**
- ☐ **2 teaspoons chopped fresh basil**
- ☐ **1 tablespoon chopped fresh parsley**
- ☐ **125 mL (4 fl oz) virgin olive oil**
- ☐ **ground black pepper**

Combine olives, anchovy fillets, Parmesan cheese, walnuts, oregano, basil and parsley in a bowl. Gradually mix in olive oil, until a thin smooth paste is formed. Stand for 1 hour. Season with black pepper. Store in refrigerator for up to 5 days.

Bowls Lifestyle Imports *Bottles* Italia Line 2002 *Statue* Saywell

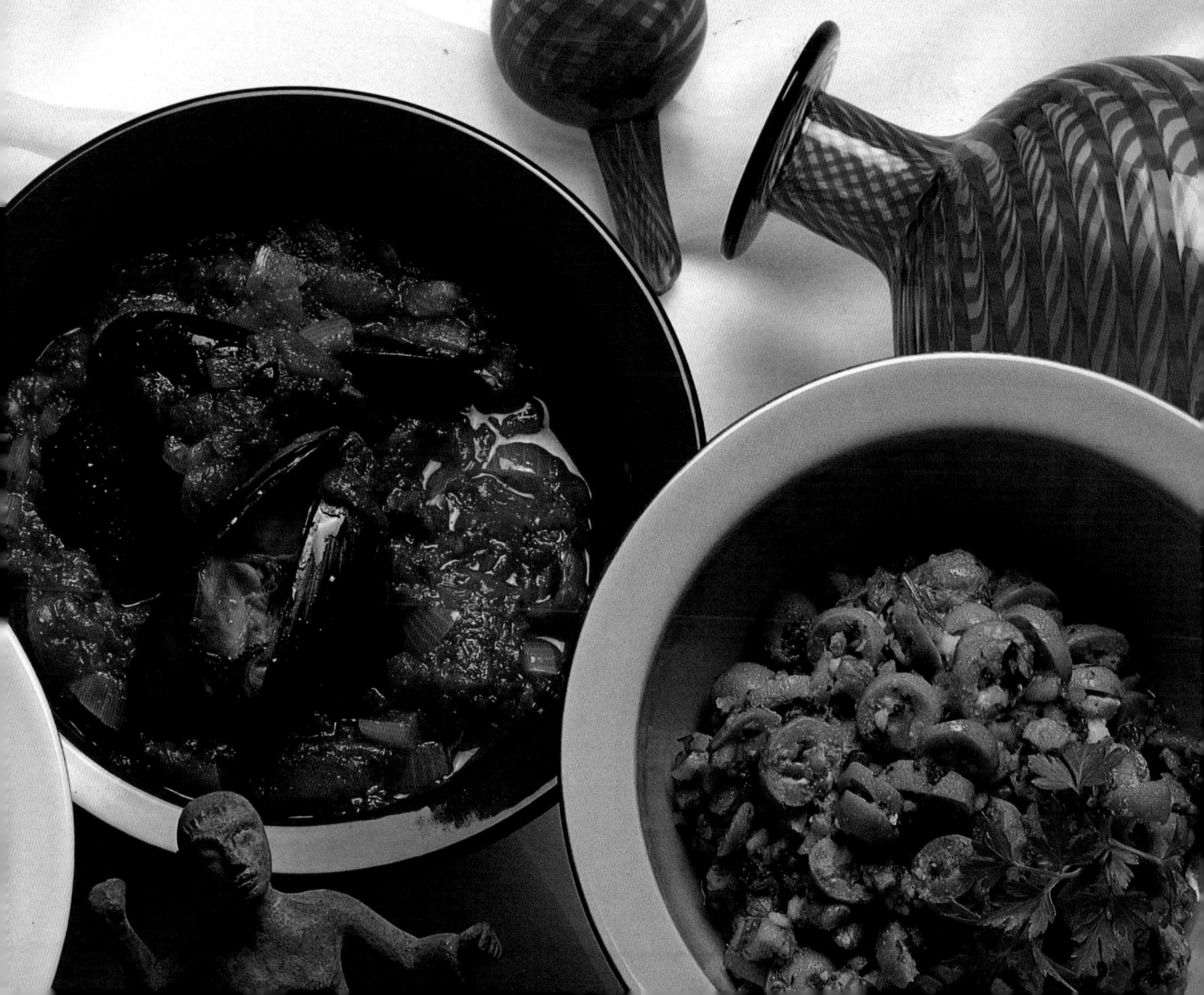

SEAFOOD CANNELLONI WITH SAFFRON SAUCE

Serves 4

- ☐ 8 lasagne sheets, blanched, 13 x 16 cm (5 x 6¹/₂ in) cooked size

FILLING
- ☐ 30 g (1 oz) butter
- ☐ 315 g (10 oz) firm-fleshed fish fillets, cut into bite size pieces
- ☐ 280 g (9 oz) scallops, cut into bite size pieces
- ☐ ground white pepper
- ☐ fresh lemon juice
- ☐ 315 g (10 oz) ricotta cheese, drained
- ☐ 1 egg, lightly beaten
- ☐ 1 teaspoon finely chopped fresh parsley
- ☐ 1 teaspoon snipped fresh chives
- ☐ ground (grated) nutmeg

SAUCE
- ☐ 30 g (1 oz) butter
- ☐ 1 tablespoon finely chopped onion
- ☐ 1 clove garlic, crushed
- ☐ 1-2 x 1 g sachets pure saffron powder
- ☐ 300 mL (9¹/₂ fl oz) cream (single)
- ☐ ground white pepper

1 To make filling, melt butter in a saucepan and cook fish and scallops for 4-5 minutes or until just opaque. Season to taste with white pepper and lemon juice. Transfer to a bowl using a slotted spoon. Pour off pan juices and reserve. Place seafood mixture, ricotta cheese, egg, parsley and chives in a bowl. Season to taste with nutmeg. Mix to combine.

2 To make sauce, melt butter in a pan and cook onion and garlic for 4-5 minutes. Add saffron to taste and cook for 1 minute, then pour in cream and reserved seafood juices and season to taste with white pepper. Bring to the boil. Reduce heat and simmer, stirring occasionally, for 5 minutes or until sauce thickens slightly. Strain and discard any solids.

3 To make cannelloni, place some filling down centre of each pasta sheet. Roll up to form a thick tube. Arrange cannelloni in a greased ovenproof dish, pour sauce over and cover with foil. Bake at 180°C (350°F/Gas 4) for 20 minutes or until heated through. Serve immediately.

Seafood Cannelloni with Saffron Sauce, Tuna and Red Pepper Filled Shells, Pork and Sage Filled Ravioli

Plates and Decanter Villeroy & Boch Fabric Potpourri

PORK AND SAGE FILLED RAVIOLI

Serves 6

PASTA
- ☐ 410 g (13 oz) plain flour
- ☐ pinch salt
- ☐ 4 eggs, lightly beaten
- ☐ 1 egg yolk, beaten with 1 tablespoon water
- ☐ grated fresh Parmesan cheese

FILLING
- ☐ 315 g (10 oz) ricotta cheese, drained
- ☐ 60 g (2 oz) lean bacon, finely chopped
- ☐ 155 g (5 oz) lean cooked pork, finely diced
- ☐ ¹/₂ teaspoon finely chopped fresh parsley
- ☐ ¹/₂ teaspoon finely chopped fresh sage
- ☐ 1 teaspoon grated fresh Parmesan cheese
- ☐ ground (grated) nutmeg
- ☐ freshly ground black pepper

1 To make pasta, combine flour and salt in a pile on work surface. Form a well in centre, add eggs and begin working into flour using a fork or your fingers. Continue

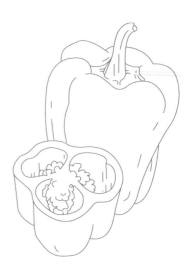

TUNA AND RED PEPPER FILLED SHELLS

These filled shells are fun to eat hot or cold as finger food, or they can be served with a sauce as a first course.

Makes 16 filled shells

- ☐ **16 giant pasta shells**

FILLING
- ☐ **250 g (8 oz) ricotta cheese, drained**
- ☐ **440 g (14 oz) canned tuna in brine, drained and flaked**
- ☐ **$^1/_2$ red pepper, diced**
- ☐ **1 tablespoon chopped capers**
- ☐ **1 teaspoon snipped fresh chives**
- ☐ **4 tablespoons grated cheddar or Swiss cheese**
- ☐ **pinch ground (grated) nutmeg**
- ☐ **freshly ground black pepper**
- ☐ **2 tablespoons grated fresh Parmesan cheese**

1   Cook 8 pasta shells in a large saucepan of boiling water until al dente. Drain, rinse under cold water and drain again. Set aside, not overlapping. Repeat with remaining shells.

2   To make filling, place ricotta cheese and tuna in a bowl and mix to combine. Mix in red pepper, capers, chives, 2 tablespoons grated cheese, nutmeg, and pepper to taste.

3   Fill each shell with ricotta mixture, and place in a shallow ovenproof dish. Sprinkle with remaining grated cheese and Parmesan cheese. Place under a preheated grill and cook until cheese melts.

until the dough holds together. Knead with hands for 5-6 minutes, or until a smooth, elastic dough forms. Add extra flour or a little water if necessary. Cover dough with plastic food wrap or a damp cloth and set aside to rest at room temperature for 30 minutes. Divide dough into four portions. Working with one portion at a time, roll out on a floured board to form thin, rectangular sheets of pasta. Cover sheets with plastic food wrap and rest for 10 minutes.

2   To make filling, place ricotta cheese, bacon, pork, parsley, sage and Parmesan cheese in a bowl. Mix to combine and season to taste with nutmeg and black pepper.

3   Working with one sheet of pasta at a time, cut pasta into rectangles 4 x 8 cm (1$^1/_2$ x 3 in). Place a teaspoon of filling just off centre of each rectangle and brush edges with egg and water mixture. Fold pasta over to encase filling. Press edges together and trim with a zigzag pastry wheel. Place in a single layer on a tray and repeat with remaining pasta and filling.

4   Cook ravioli, a few at a time, in boiling water in a large saucepan for 4 minutes or until al dente. Drain and keep warm. To serve, sprinkle with Parmesan cheese.

PAPPARDELLE WITH PEAS AND BACON

Pappardelle is a strong pasta which goes with rich sauces. It is ideal to serve with game.

Serves 4

- ☐ **60 g (2 oz) butter**
- ☐ **1 onion, sliced**
- ☐ **1 clove garlic, crushed**
- ☐ **pinch chilli flakes, or to taste**
- ☐ **3 bacon rashers, chopped**
- ☐ **90 g (3 oz) shelled peas, blanched**
- ☐ **1 teaspoon finely chopped fresh mint**
- ☐ **1 tablespoon finely chopped fresh parsley**
- ☐ **freshly ground black pepper**
- ☐ **500 g (1 lb) fresh pappardelle, or 410 g (13 oz) dried**
- ☐ **2 eggs, lightly beaten**
- ☐ **90 mL (3 fl oz) cream (single)**
- ☐ **1¹/₂ tablespoons grated fresh pecorino cheese**

1　Melt butter in a large frypan and cook onion, garlic and chilli for 6-8 minutes. Add bacon and cook for 5 minutes longer. Stir in peas, mint and 2 teaspoons parsley.

Season to taste with black pepper. Set aside and keep warm.

2　Cook pappardelle in boiling water in a large saucepan until al dente. Drain, then add to pea mixture, toss lightly to coat and remove from heat. Combine eggs, cream, pecorino and remaining parsley and stir into pasta mixture. Serve as soon as eggs begin to set and cling to pasta – this will take only a few seconds. The sauce should be slightly runny.

❖

SPIRELLI WITH HAM AND ARTICHOKES

Serves 4

- ☐ **500 g (1 lb) fresh spirelli, or 410 g (13 oz) dried spirelli**
- ☐ **2 teaspoons olive oil**
- ☐ **315 g (10 oz) ham, cut into strips**
- ☐ **6 canned artichoke hearts, sliced lengthways**
- ☐ **3 eggs, beaten with 1 tablespoon grated fresh Parmesan cheese**
- ☐ **freshly ground black pepper**

1　Cook spirelli in boiling water in a large saucepan following packet directions or until al dente. Drain, set aside and keep warm.

2　Heat oil in a frypan and cook ham and artichoke hearts for 1-2 minutes.

3　Add pasta and toss to combine. Remove from heat and quickly stir in egg mixture. Season to taste with black pepper. Serve as soon as the eggs start to stick to spirelli – this will take only a few seconds.

Pappardelle with Peas and Bacon, Chicken Livers and Mushrooms on Spaghetti

Fabric J. Redelman *Plate* Villeroy & Boch

Fabrics J. Redelman Plates Lifestyle Imports Cruet Set Zyliss

FETTUCCINE WITH VEAL CREAM SAUCE

Serves 4

- ☐ **500 g (1 lb) fresh fettuccine, or 410 g (13 oz) dried fettuccine**
- ☐ **1 tablespoon olive oil**
- ☐ **500 g (1 lb) thin veal steaks, cut into strips**
- ☐ **1 clove garlic, crushed**
- ☐ **1 teaspoon chopped fresh parsley**
- ☐ **2 teaspoons paprika**
- ☐ **1¹/₂ tablespoons brandy**
- ☐ **2 tablespoons concentrated tomato paste**
- ☐ **410 g (13 oz) thick sour cream**
- ☐ **freshly ground black pepper**

1   Cook fettuccine in boiling water in a large saucepan until al dente. Drain, set aside and keep warm.

2   Heat oil in a large frypan and cook veal for 3-4 minutes or until browned. Add garlic, parsley and paprika and cook for 1-2 minutes longer. Stir in brandy and cook until evaporated. Whisk in tomato paste and sour cream. Season to taste with black pepper and bring to the boil. Reduce heat and simmer until sauce reduces and thickens. Stir in pasta and toss to coat.

CHICKEN LIVERS AND MUSHROOMS ON SPAGHETTI

A variation of a sauce created for the great singer Caruso.

Serves 4

- ☐ **500 g (1 lb) fresh spaghetti, or 400 g (13 oz) dried spaghetti**
- ☐ **1 tablespoon vegetable oil**
- ☐ **90 g (3 oz) grated fresh Parmesan cheese**

TOMATO SAUCE
- ☐ **1 tablespoon vegetable oil**
- ☐ **30 g (1 oz) butter**
- ☐ **1 onion, finely diced**
- ☐ **2 cloves garlic, crushed**
- ☐ **12 small button mushrooms, halved**
- ☐ **440 g (14 oz) canned Italian peeled tomatoes, undrained and mashed**
- ☐ **1 teaspoon sugar**
- ☐ **300 mL (9¹/₂ oz) chicken stock**
- ☐ **ground black pepper**

CHICKEN LIVER SAUCE
- ☐ **30 g (1 oz) butter**
- ☐ **250 g (8 oz) chicken livers, trimmed and sliced**
- ☐ **1 teaspoon finely chopped fresh thyme, or ¹/₄ teaspoon dried thyme**
- ☐ **90 mL (3 fl oz) Marsala**
- ☐ **1 tablespoon finely chopped fresh parsley**

1   To make Tomato Sauce, heat oil and butter in a frypan, and cook onion until soft. Add garlic and mushrooms and cook for 2-3 minutes longer. Combine tomatoes and sugar and add to mushrooms. Cook over a low heat for 10 minutes. Stir in stock and simmer for 30 minutes longer or until sauce reduces and thickens. Season to taste with black pepper.

2   To make Chicken Liver Sauce, melt butter in a saucepan and cook chicken livers and thyme over a medium heat until brown. Increase heat, stir in Marsala and cook for 1-2 minutes. Stir in parsley.

3   Cook spaghetti in boiling water in a large saucepan until al dente. Drain and fold through oil.

4   Arrange half spaghetti on a warm serving platter, top with half chicken liver mixture, then half Tomato Sauce. Sprinkle over half Parmesan cheese, then repeat layers. Serve immediately.

Fettuccine with Veal Cream Sauce, Spirelli with Ham and Artichokes

BAKED PENNE AND FRESH TUNA

Partially cooking pasta, mixing it with other ingredients and then baking it in the oven is a wonderful way of trapping flavours. If fresh tuna is unavailable, any firm-fleshed fish may be used instead.

Serves 4

- ☐ **350 g (11 oz) dried penne, or other short pasta**

TUNA SAUCE
- ☐ **2 zucchini (courgettes), sliced**
- ☐ **salt**
- ☐ **200 g (6¹/₂ oz) butter**
- ☐ **350 g (11 oz) fresh tuna, cut into chunks**
- ☐ **2 tablespoons plain flour**
- ☐ **250 mL (8 fl oz) milk**
- ☐ **freshly ground black pepper**
- ☐ **ground (grated) nutmeg**
- ☐ **200 g (6¹/₂ oz) grated fresh Parmesan cheese**
- ☐ **155 g (5 oz) grated mozzarella cheese**

1 To make sauce, sprinkle zucchini (courgettes) with salt and place in a colander or sieve. Set aside to drain for 30 minutes. Rinse and pat dry with absorbent kitchen paper. Melt 30 g (1 oz) butter in a frypan and cook zucchini (courgettes) and tuna until flesh turns white. Remove zucchini (courgettes) and tuna from pan and set aside. Reserve pan juices.

2 Melt 30 g (1 oz) butter in a saucepan, add flour and cook for 1-2 minutes. Remove from heat and gradually blend in reserved pan juices and milk. Cook over a medium heat, stirring constantly, until sauce boils and thickens. Season to taste with black pepper and nutmeg. Stir in half the Parmesan cheese and toss through zucchini (courgettes) and tuna.

3 Cook pasta in boiling water in a large saucepan for half the time stated on packet. Drain and stir into sauce.

4 Place one-third pasta mixture in a greased ovenproof dish. Cover with one-third remaining Parmesan and one-third mozzarella. Dot with one third remaining butter. Repeat with remaining pasta mixture, cheese and butter, finishing with butter. Grind black pepper across top and bake at 220°C (425°F/Gas 7) for 20 minutes.

Baked Penne and Fresh Tuna, Pasta Parcels with Gorgonzola Sauce, Spaghetti with Salami and Tomato Sauce

PASTA PARCELS WITH GORGONZOLA SAUCE

This eye-catching dish can be prepared up to three hours in advance, and is delicious served at room temperature for a summer luncheon.

Serves 8

- ☐ **8 spinach lasagne sheets, approximately 16 cm (6¹/₂ in) square, cooked**

FILLING
- ☐ **500 g (1 lb) fresh spinach, stalks removed, leaves blanched and squeezed to remove excess water**
- ☐ **4 hard-boiled eggs, chopped**
- ☐ **125 g (4 oz) prosciutto, finely chopped**
- ☐ **1 tablespoon finely chopped red onion**
- ☐ **1 clove garlic, crushed**
- ☐ **freshly ground black pepper**

SAUCE
- ☐ **100 g (3¹/₂ oz) Gorgonzola cheese**
- ☐ **375 mL (12 fl oz) cream (single)**
- ☐ **1¹/₂ tablespoons Dijon-style mustard**
- ☐ **3-4 tablespoons lemon juice**
- ☐ **2 tablespoons chopped hazelnuts, roasted**

1 To make filling, shred spinach finely. Place spinach, hard-boiled eggs, prosciutto, onion and garlic in a bowl. Toss to combine and season to taste with black pepper.

2 To make sauce, place Gorgonzola cheese and cream in a food processor or blender and process until smooth. Add mustard and lemon juice to taste and process until well blended, then stir in hazelnuts.

3 To assemble parcels, divide filling between lasagne sheets, forming a mound in centre of each sheet. Fold corners of pasta in like an envelope to form a parcel. Transfer parcels to a shallow ovenproof dish. Spoon sauce over, cover with foil and bake at 180°C (350°F/Gas 4) for 20 minutes or until heated through.

COOK'S TIP
Odds and ends of pasta in your cupboard or pantry can be combined to make a delicious pasta soup or add them to a vegetable or meat soup to extend it.

SPAGHETTI WITH SALAMI AND TOMATO SAUCE

Serves 4

- ☐ **1 medium eggplant (aubergine), cut into 2.5 cm (1 in) cubes**
- ☐ **salt**
- ☐ **olive oil**
- ☐ **1 small onion, sliced lengthways**
- ☐ **1 small red pepper, cut into short strips**
- ☐ **2 small zucchini (courgettes), sliced**
- ☐ **440 g (14 oz) canned Italian peeled tomatoes, undrained and mashed**
- ☐ **freshly ground black pepper**
- ☐ **125 g (4 oz) salami, cut into small cubes**
- ☐ **500 g (1 lb) dried wholemeal spaghetti**
- ☐ **8-10 small Ligurian or Nicoise olives**
- ☐ **grated fresh Parmesan cheese**

1 Sprinkle eggplant (aubergine) with salt and place in a colander to drain. Heat a little olive oil in a frypan and gently cook onion, red pepper and zucchini (courgettes) for 4-5 minutes or until onion softens. Remove from pan and set aside. Rinse eggplant (aubergine) under cold running water, then pat dry with absorbent kitchen paper. Add a little more olive oil to pan and cook eggplant (aubergine) until golden. Pour off any excess oil and return onion mixture to pan.

2 Add tomatoes and season to taste with black pepper. Cook over a low heat, stirring occasionally, for 10 minutes. Mix salami through.

3 Cook spaghetti in a large saucepan of boiling water following packet instructions. Drain, transfer to a warmed serving platter, spoon hot sauce over, then sprinkle with olives and Parmesan cheese.

PASTA PERFECTION

What sort of pasta should you buy? What's the best way to cook it? How much should you cook per person? How can you make your own? This chapter will show you how to master the art of pasta cooking.

Think of Italian food and you think of pasta. It is such a part of Italian culinary history - they were writing about it fifteen centuries ago - that we tend to think of it as solely theirs. Some form of pasta, that is a boiled dough of flour and water, was a staple food for many early civilisations. It would have to be the next step after discovering flour!

Even today pasta costs very little, is easily prepared, versatile and filling. We now know what was probably always taken for granted – pasta is good for us. It is high in protein, low in sodium and fat, contains vitamins, iron, minerals, fibre and uses no preservatives. Whether it is simply boiled and served with a splash of olive oil and garlic, or formed into a more intricate baked dish, it is never boring.

Buying Pasta

✧ Nowadays pasta is available in a number of guises.
✧ Convenience of handling and storage, texture and flavour, and good cooking properties will all contribute to your choice.
✧ Packaged dried pasta, pasta asciutto, comes imported or locally made. It is made from durum wheat semolina and water, labelled pasta di semolina di grana duro in Italian. Eggs are sometimes used, in which case it is marked on the packet, all'uovo on imported brands.
✧ Dried pasta needs to rehydrate as well as cook, therefore a longer cooking time is required.

✧ Commercial fresh pasta, pasta fresca, is soft and pliable and is usually sold loose. It has the combined flavours of both durum wheat semolina and eggs. Being fresh, it needs a very short cooking time but it has a short life of 3-5 days.
✧ Pre-packed dry 'fresh' pasta uses eggs. It too should be made from durum wheat semolina and labelled accordingly.
✧ Durum wheat is a species of 'hard' wheat, so-called because it has an endosperm rich in gluten. It has a distinctive nutty flavour and a rich amber colour. When milled to a semolina (a coarsely ground meal), and mixed with water, the resulting dough has some unique characteristics ideal for commercial pasta.
✧ Pasta comes in the most confusing array of shapes and sizes.
✧ Many shapes are interchangeable and half the appeal of pasta is inventing your own combinations of pasta and sauce.
✧ However, regional traditions should not be ignored. There are logical reasons for putting a Bolognese ragu on spaghetti, for instance.
✧ As a general rule, thin, long pasta needs a good clinging sauce, hollow or twisted shapes take chunky sauces, wide, flat noodles carry rich sauces and delicate shapes require a light sauce without large pieces in it.

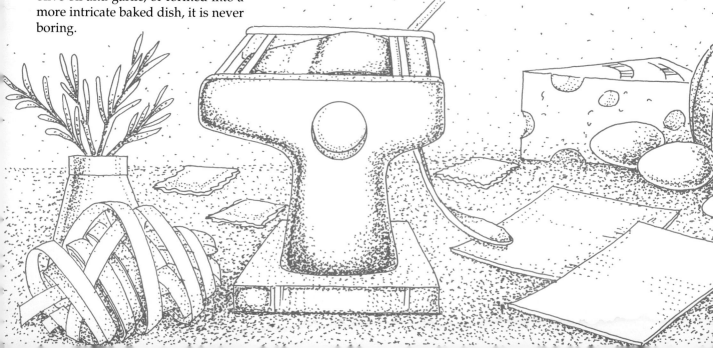

COOKING PASTA

✧ Cook pasta in a large, deep saucepan of water. The general rule is 1 litre (1¾ pt) to 100 g (3½ oz) pasta. Bring water to a rolling boil, toss in salt to taste (in Italy 1 tablespoon per every 100 g (3½ oz) pasta is usual), then stir in pasta. If you wish, add some oil. When water comes back to the boil, begin timing. The pasta is done when it is 'al dente', that is tender but with resistance to the bite. Remove pasta from water by straining through a colander or lifting out of saucepan with tongs or a fork.

✧ Never rinse pasta, unless it is to be used for a cold salad. The pasta is now ready for the sauce.

✧ Stir through a little oil or melted butter and serve, topped with sauce, or toss pasta straight into sauce. Italians call this method 'strascicate' and it is a quick and easy way of evenly distributing the sauce before serving.

HOW MUCH TO COOK?			
	PASTA TYPE	FIRST COURSE	MAIN MEAL
PER SERVE	Dried pasta	60-75 g (2-2½ oz)	75-100 g (2½-3½ oz)
	Fresh pasta	75-100 g (2½-3½ oz)	125-155 g (4-5 oz)
	Filled pasta (such as ravioli)	155-185 g (5-6 oz)	185-200 g (6-6½ oz)

REHEATING COOKED PASTA

✧ Reheating pasta can be done successfully, if it is already combined with a sauce.

✧ To reheat, place in a greased, ovenproof dish, cover with foil, and reheat in a moderate oven.

✧ Pasta which has been cooked and coated with oil can be heated by placing in an oiled ovenproof dish, covered with a damp tea-towel and then reheated in a slow to moderate oven for 15-20 minutes.

✧ Alternatively, the pasta and sauce may be stirred together in a frying pan just long enough to heat through.

✧ Leftover pasta can be reheated and served as delicious snacks or appetisers. The microwave is the ideal way to reheat cooked pasta dishes; just cover and reheat on HIGH (100%) for 1-2 minutes per serve.

✧ Spaghetti and pesto sauce can be mixed with eggs and then cooked to make a delicious omelette.

✧ Leftover pasta and sauces can be mixed together then cooked in olive oil to make a crisp thick pancake.

HOMEMADE PASTA

❖

BASIC PASTA DOUGH

A general rule to follow when making pasta is: 1 large egg to every 100 g (3¹/₂ oz) flour, and 100 g (3¹/₂ oz) flour per person for a main course serve.

Serves 4

- ☐ **410 g (13 oz) plain flour**
- ☐ **4 large eggs**
- ☐ **large pinch salt**
- ☐ **some water**

1 Pile flour in a mound on a work surface. Make a well in the centre. Break in eggs, add salt and, using a fork first and then your hands, incorporate eggs into flour to form a coarse dough.
2 Place dough in a food processor or knead by hand. If necessary, cautiously add extra flour or water as the case may be. Continue to knead until a smooth, elastic dough is formed, this will take 6-8 minutes. If using the food processor do the last 2-3 minutes of kneading by hand.
3 Cover dough well with a dry cloth and set aside to rest for at least 15 minutes at room temperature.
4 Divide dough into manageable sections. Keep dough you are not working with covered with a dry cloth. Take one piece of dough at a time and press it out using the ball of your hand. Begin to roll out gently using a long rolling pin and a little flour to form a flat sheet of pasta 3-5 mm (¹/₈-¹/₄ in) thick, for cut pastas and lasagne, or 2 mm (¹/₁₆) for stuffed pasta.
5 If making pasta for ravioli, begin to make them straight away as the pasta needs to be moist for the edges to seal together. If it is to be cut into shapes or lengths, leave sheets out to dry slightly before proceeding. To cut into lengths such as fettuccine, roll up each sheet of pasta lengthways. Using a very sharp knife cut the roll into slices of appropriate widths. Cut pasta for fettuccine into 1.15 cm (¹/₂ in) widths.

Flavoured Pasta

There are any number of ingredients (savoury or sweet) that can be used to give pasta colour and flavour. Because many of these additives contain liquid or have 'short' qualities, the dough may be harder to work once you begin kneading. A little extra flour or water, as necessary, will adjust the balance.

❖

TOMATO PASTA

- ☐ **3 large eggs**
- ☐ **2¹/₂ tablespoons concentrated tomato paste**
- ☐ **410 g (13 oz) plain flour, sifted**

Beat tomato paste into eggs, then follow method as for making Basic Pasta Dough.

❖

CHOCOLATE PASTA

- ☐ **3 large eggs**
- ☐ **1 tablespoon cocoa powder**
- ☐ **410 g (13 oz) plain flour, sifted**

PASTA-MAKING HINTS

✧ Making pasta at home is not difficult, particularly for those accustomed to making their own pastry. No special equipment is needed, a large flat surface for rolling and a rolling pin are the only neccessities.
✧ A hand-cranked pasta machine helps to make pasta of an even thickness and cuts it quickly and neatly.
✧ As well as the pleasure of making it yourself, an advantage of home-made pasta is the range of shapes and flavours you can create.
✧ Homemade pasta, however, does not dry successfully, as the high moisture content makes the pasta dry out too quickly and crack.

Beat cocoa powder into eggs, then follow method as for making Basic Pasta Dough.

❖

SPINACH PASTA

- ☐ **3 large eggs**
- ☐ **75 g (2¹/₂ oz) cooked, thoroughly drained and pureed spinach**
- ☐ **large pinch salt**
- ☐ **pinch ground (grated) nutmeg**
- ☐ **pinch white pepper**
- ☐ **410 g (13 oz) plain flour, sifted**

Combine eggs with spinach, salt, nutmeg and white pepper, then follow method as for Basic Pasta Dough.

Pile flour in a mound on a work surface. Make a well in the centre and break in eggs.

Knead by hand, until the dough is smooth and elastic. When kneading push the dough away from you using the heel of your hand.

Divide dough into manageable sections. Take one piece of dough at a time and press it out using the ball of your hand, then roll out gently using a long rolling pin.

Making Filled Pasta

Make the pasta as for Basic Pasta Dough in the preceding recipes (page 36). It should be used as soon as it is made to avoid drying out, so it is important to make the filling first and to have it waiting for the pasta.

Using a mould: These trays come in a selection of prepressed ravioli shapes, accompanied by a little rolling pin. The moulds give a ravioli of uniform shape and size.

Folding by hand: Make the pasta following the Basic Pasta Dough recipe. Work with one sheet of pasta at a time, keeping the rest well covered. Cut each sheet into the required shapes. For square ravioli cut out rectangles, for agnolotti (half moon shapes) cut out circles, and for rectangles, cut out squares. Brush edges with beaten egg. Working with one shape at a time, put some filling off-side of centre, then fold the other side over it, matching the outside edges. Press together firmly, then go around edges with a pastry cutter to neaten them and give a tight seal.

Filling a sheet at a time: Cut two sheets of pasta into rectangles, one slightly larger than the other. Place the smaller sheet on a large flat surface and place equal amounts of filling on it at regular intervals. Starting at one end, position the larger sheet of pasta over the smaller one. Pressing the sheets together as you go. When each sheet is completed, run a finger around the mounds of filling and along the cutting lines, to press the sheets together. Now cut the sealed lines using a floured pastry wheel, zigzag cutter or knife. Homemade ravioli may be frozen. To freeze, place ravioli in single layers and not overlapping, in a rigid container.

USING A PASTA MACHINE

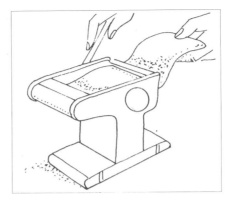

Step 1
Make dough as for Step 1 of Basic Pasta Dough and divide dough into manageable pieces. Set the rollers of the pasta machine on its widest setting and feed the dough through.

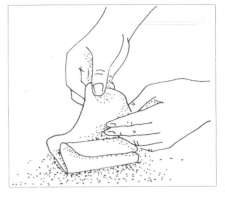

Step 2
Fold the rolled dough into quarters to make a square.

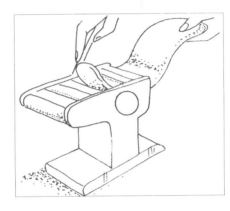

Step 3
Feed the dough through the machine again, then fold as for Step 2. Repeat folding and rolling of dough 4-5 times until you have a shiny, smooth and elastic dough.

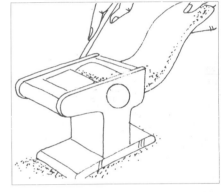

Step 4
Close the rollers a notch at a time and roll the dough thinner and thinner until the desired thickness is reached. Set aside to dry for 10-15 minutes.

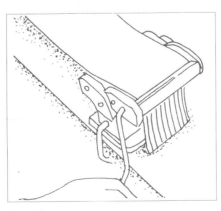

Step 5
To cut, using pasta machine, feed each strip of pasta through the appropriate blades.

Step 6
As the strips of dough emerge from the machine catch them on your hand.

COMMON PASTA TYPES AND SHAPES

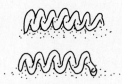

fusilli; spirals or springs

gnocchi; shell-shaped, like a smooth conchiglie

lasagne; flat sheets of pasta

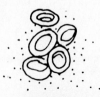

anelli; small rings usually used in soups

bucatini; hollow spaghetti

ditali; thimbles. Small hollow rounds

ditalini; a smaller version of ditali

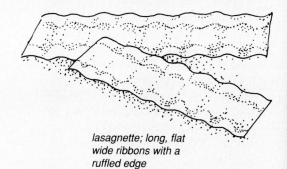

lasagnette; long, flat wide ribbons with a ruffled edge

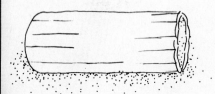

cannelloni; large tubular shapes for stuffing

capelli d'angelo; angel's hair. Long, extremely thin pasta

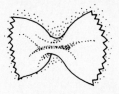

farfalle; bows or butterflies

The suffix
-ini indicates a smaller version,
-oni means larger,
-rigate means ridged, while
-lisce means smooth.

linguine; thin, narrow ribbon pasta

macaroni; generic term applying to a number of hollow shapes

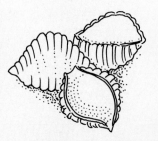

conchiglie; shells. From very tiny, to giant ones for stuffing

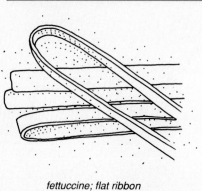

fettuccine; flat ribbon pasta

orecchiette; small ear-shaped pasta

risoni; rice-shaped pasta

rotelli; either wheel-shaped, or a hollow spiral

spaghetti; meaning 'string'. Thin circular ribbon pasta

agnolotti; half-moon shaped

cappelletti; hat-shaped

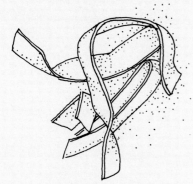

pappardelle; very wide ribbon pasta

spirelli; spiral or cork-screw shaped

ravioli; squares

penne; short tubular shapes, angle-cut at the ends

quadrucci; small flat squares of lasagne

tortellini; folded to form a hole in the middle

tagliatelle; flat ribbon pasta, similar to fettuccine

vermicelli; a thin, circular ribbon pasta

ziti; tubular shapes. A version of macaroni

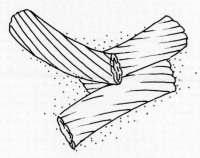

rigatoni; ridged hollow shape

THE ITALIAN HERB GARDEN

Where would Italian food be without those sprigs of rosemary, dashes of oregano or generous helpings of fresh sweet basil? Growing your own herbs will not only save you time and money, it will open the door to the true flavour of Italy.

No Italian kitchen is without fresh or dried bunches of basil, bay leaves, oregano, parsley, sage, rosemary and thyme. Italy is a country whose repertory of herbs is large and of high quality. All are aromatic in the garden and indispensable in the kitchen.

An Italian herb garden need not be large. It should be enclosed or in a sheltered position with the plants well spaced. The best site is a sunny open position with a well-drained soil and protection from strong winds and heavy frosts. The size of the garden can be adjusted to suit your site, but try to choose an area within easy reach of the kitchen. Some plants such as basil, parsley, marjoram, mint and thyme are especially suitable for growing in individual containers.

When making your Italian herb garden, the first step is to prepare the soil. The best fertiliser for herbs is compost or well-rotted manure. This should be dug or mixed well into the soil at planting time. Place taller-growing plants at the back so as not to smother the short or creeping herbs. Water well until the plants are established. Herb gardens need to be accessible and are best arranged in plots divided by paths of brick, stone or gravel.

Basil (basilico)

Basil originally came from India where it is still regarded as a sacred herb. It was known in ancient times in Southern Europe, and in Italy it symbolised love. Traditionally, a pot of basil was placed in the window by a girl as an invitation to her lover to call on her.

Basil is the most important herb in Italian cooking. There are many different types of basil, but the most commonly used is the sweet basil, *Ocimum basilicum*, whose large, shiny bright green leaves are quick to give off a delicious spicy and aromatic scent at the slightest touch.

A compact form known as bush basil has smaller leaves, is milder in flavour, and makes neat little pot plants. Dark opal, with its highly aromatic purple leaves, is popular as an ornamental plant and makes wonderful deep pink basil vinegar.

The lettuce-leaved basil has large crinkly leaves ideal for tearing up and tossing in a mixed green salad.

Basil is grown as an annual from seed. Sow seeds in spring when the likelihood of frost has passed, or grow indoors and transplant. Seeds germinate in about seven days. Basil needs a sunny position and a well-drained soil. Once established, pick the tops out constantly. This will make the plants branch and produce more leaves as well as preventing them from flowering and going to seed too soon. In the garden, basil is a good companion with tomatoes.

Bay leaves (alloro, lauro)

The bay tree, *Laurus nobilis*, makes a very attractive addition to any garden. As it is very slow to grow, it is particularly good for potting and decorating a courtyard or terrace. The dark green leaves can be picked from an established plant at any time, and possess a wonderful warm aroma that complements cooked tomato dishes, soups, stews and casseroles.

It is native to the Mediterranean region and will eventually reach 15 m (45 ft) tall in the garden in warm frost-free climates. It prefers a fairly rich soil, good drainage and a sunny open position. In cooler areas it will grow only as a tall shrub and will need the protection of the greenhouse, or the indoors, during winter.

Florence fennel (finocchio)

Florence fennel, *Foeniculum vulgare* var. *dulce,* is a compact annual plant grown for its swollen base. It is eaten as a vegetable in Italy both raw and cooked in the same way as celery. It is a variant of sweet fennel *F. vulgare,* a robust perennial plant generally used as a fish herb in other parts of Europe.

Florence fennel needs a good rich, well-drained soil and requires regular watering during dry periods. As the plant needs warm weather for the base to fill out, it is best to sow seed in late spring or early summer. Thin seedlings to stand 20 cm (8 in) apart. When the plants are around 30 cm (12 in) high, or when the base is the size of an egg, draw the soil up around the bulbs to blanch them. In two or three weeks the plant is ready for use.

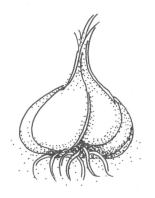

Garlic (aglio)

Garlic is a classic ingredient in Italian cuisine especially in dishes originating in the south, particularly around Naples. There is no substitute for the delicious flavour of fresh garlic in cooking. By stimulating the gastric juices, garlic acts both as an appetiser and a digestive.

It is an easy herb to grow and is propagated by individual cloves planted in early spring at a depth of 4 cm (1½ in). Plants thrive best in a humus-enriched, moist but well-drained soil. The bulbs are carefully lifted in late summer when the leaves have withered and started to fall over. Dry in a cool, airy place. When dry, the tops are traditionally braided together and hung up ready for use.

Marjoram (maggiorana)

Also known as knotted or sweet marjoram, marjoram, *Origanum majorana,* is a delightful perennial plant which is grown as an annual in cold climates. It grows to a height of 20 cm (8 in) high and has very small greyish-green oval leaves which have a fresh, fragrant aroma. They are used to flavour many meat and fish dishes, soups and stews.

Grow marjoram in a rich, well-drained soil in full sun. To prevent the plant from becoming leggy, cut when the flower is just coming into bloom. This is also the best time to capture the full fragrance of the plant when harvesting for drying.

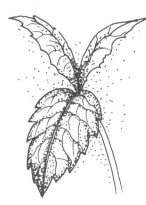

Mint (menta)

The most common variety of mint used in Italian cooking is spearmint, *Mentha spicata.* It is a creeping perennial plant, to 60 cm (24 in) high, with long, spearlike leaves and a refreshing, clean aroma used to flavour salads, soups, vegetables and fish dishes.

In the garden, mint requires a rich moist soil and partial shade. The plant will spread rapidly by underground stems. To contain invasive growth, keep mint in a bottomless container set in the ground. Trim the plant regularly to encourage bushy and better growth.

Oregano (oregano)

Oregano, *Origanum vulgare,* is the wild form of marjoram. It can be seen growing wild in countries bordering the Mediterranean and is abundant in southern Italy. Fresh or dried, it appears in many Italian dishes and goes particularly well with tomatoes, cooked cheese dishes, sauces, and as a topping for pizzas.

Oregano is a robust perennial plant to 70 cm (28 in) high which spreads by underground stems. The entire plant is hairy with thickly set small oval-shaped leaves. It grows best in a sunny, well-drained position and benefits from a regular trim to encourage compact growth.

Parsley (prezzemolo)

Parsley, *Petroselinum crispum*, is native to the Mediterranean region and is thought to have originated on the island of Sardinia. There are several varieties, but the type most commonly used in Italian cooking is the flat-leaved parsley. It is also known as Italian parsley.

Parsley is biennial and flowers in its second year. The seed is very slow to germinate, but is best sown where it is to grow. Choose a partially shaded position in a moderately rich, moisture-retaining soil. Soak seeds in warm water overnight before planting in spring. Cover seed with a light covering of fine soil and keep moist. Thin seedlings to stand around 20 cm (8 in) apart. Parsley leaves should always be picked from the outside, allowing the new leaves to grow from the middle of the plant. Removing the flowering heads in the second year helps prolong the life of the plant.

Rosemary (rosmarino)

A native of the Mediterranean shores, rosemary, *Rosmarinus officinalis*, is an extremely fragrant and spicy shrub that is much used by Italian cooks –

especially as a flavouring in roasts. It grows to 1.5 m (60 in) high with erect branching stems clustered with narrow leaves, green on top and silver underneath. Its delicate blue flowers appear at the tips of the branches.

Grow rosemary in a sunny, protected position with good drainage. To prevent the older branches becoming leggy, trim the bush each year taking care not to cut into the old wood. In cold climates rosemary is best cultivated in a container so that it can be moved to the protection of a glasshouse in winter.

Sage (salvia)

Sage is a native of the Mediterranean shores and has been grown and used since ancient times for its health-giving properties and to flavour food. Sage comes in numerous varieties, but the one most commonly grown for culinary purposes is the common sage, *Salvia officinalis*. It is a small woody perennial that grows to around 30 cm (12 in) high with slightly downy, oblong pointed leaves which are conspicuously veined and grey-green in colour. The leaves have a strong aromatic fragrance when crushed and are used a great deal in Italian cooking.

Grow sage in a sunny well-drained position in a light open soil. Do not overwater. Flowering stems should be cut back each year to encourage fresh new growth. Plants eventually become woody and need renewing every three or four years.

Thyme (timo)

There are many different types of thyme, but the common thyme of Italian gardens is *Thymus vulgaris*, a small shrub-like perennial that grows to around 30 cm (12 in) high. Its pungent leaves are grey-green, tiny and dotted with scent glands. Little pink or white flowers grow in whorls at the ends of the stems.

Grow thyme in a warm, sunny position in well-drained soil. Trim after flowering to encourage compact bushy growth. Thyme is easily increased by replanting stems with a piece of root attached.

Key to Herb Garden

1 Grape Vine
2 Marjoram
3 Bay Tree
4 Mint
5 Rosemary
6 Tomatoes
7 Florence Fennel
8 Dark Opal Basil
9 Thyme
10 Oregano
11 Bush Basil Pots
12 Italian Parsley
13 Sage

1

3

13

6

4

5

7

2

8

11

9

12

10

43

OLIVES, GARLIC
and
VINEGAR

Today's lighter cooking can still take advantage of the subtle flavour of olive oil. Olives and garlic give an 'authentic' taste. Learn how to use these classic ingredients in the modern way.

Garlic in the Italian Kitchen

Although indispensable to Italian cooking, garlic is not as ubiquitous as often thought. In the north, there are many cooks and dishes that do not rely on it. Its use is more common further south where tomatoes and olive oil are basic ingredients. In many kitchens, the central greenish stem of each clove is removed as this is the part which causes bitterness (particularly if the garlic is old) and, it is believed, the bad breath associated with garlic.

When buying garlic, look for tightly packed bulbs with firm, smooth skins, and avoid those which have begun to grow shoots. The large-cloved variety tends to be milder, and the purple-skinned one is sweeter.

To store garlic, place in a dark container, covered but not airtight, in a cool, dry spot. Garlic may be minced or crushed, mixed with a little salt and olive oil, and stored in airtight containers in the refrigerator. A few cloves steeped in olive oil will flavour the oil for use in cooking or dressings. Remove the garlic after 8-10 days. You will find that the flavour is retained in the oil.

❖

GARLIC MAYONNAISE

This classic garlic mayonnaise is marvellous served with raw or lightly cooked vegetables.

Makes 250 g (8 oz)

- ☐ **6 cloves garlic, crushed**
- ☐ **2 egg yolks**
- ☐ **2 tablespoons lemon juice**
- ☐ **250 mL (8 fl oz) olive oil**
- ☐ **freshly ground black pepper**

1 Place garlic, egg yolks and lemon juice in a food processor or blender and process until combined.
2 With machine running, slowly add oil to form a thick sauce. Season to taste with black pepper.

DID YOU KNOW?

It is believed that olive trees were first brought to Italy by the Ancient Greeks. The Romans refined the art of cultivating and curing olives and also of making olive oil. It was the Romans who invented the screw press – the method of extracting oil from olives which is still the basis for olive oil production today.

Table Olives

Olive varieties are generally called after their town or district of origin, but some are named by their method of curing, and a few are actually known by their varietal names.

The range of cured olives found in shops is ever increasing, but the mainstays are:

✧ **Ligurian** (from Italy) or **Nicoise** (from France) olives are tiny and brown or black in colour. They are prized for their appearance and tasty flavour.

✧ The Greek **Kalamata** olive is purplish black and slit, which lends them to marinating.

✧ **Perlas** are black olives with a solid flesh, and are often pitted. They are not salty and are a popular cooking olive.

✧ **Dry-cured** olives are black and wrinkled and have been cured in salt. They are often marinated in oil and herbs.

✧ **Sicilian-cured** refers to large crisp green olives, sometimes cracked, which have been cured in brine.

✧ **Royal**, or **Royal Victoria** olives from Greece, vary in colour from dark tan to brown-black. They taste like a fleshy Kalamata olive.

Olive Oil

To make olive oil, the olives are picked by hand, or gathered in large nets spread under the trees, they are then washed and dried, crushed to a paste and pressed to extract the liquid. The term Cold Pressed refers to this process when carried out without generating heat, which is harmful to the oil. The oil and water are separated, and the oil is sometimes filtered. Oils which have been taken from this initial pressing can be labelled First Pressing.

The classification of the finished oil is governed by law – the main

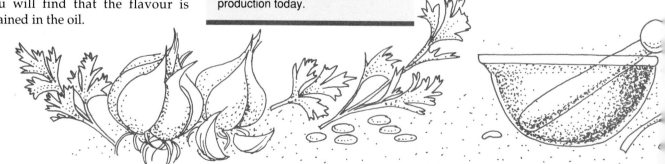

criterion being the percentage of acidity present. These gradings must be displayed on the oil's label.

✧ **Extra Virgin Olive Oil** is the top grading and must not contain more than 1 per cent acidity.

✧ **Fine Virgin Olive Oil** has a maximum acidity of 1.5 per cent.

✧ **Semi-Fine Virgin Olive Oil** has an acidity of no more than 3 per cent.

✧ **Pure Olive Oil** is a blend of Extra Virgin Olive Oil and chemically refined olive oil and has a maximum acidity of 1.5 per cent.

As climate and soil play a major part in the quality of the finished product, there are great regional differences between oils. The dry, hilly areas around the centre of Italy are said to produce the top oil, and those from Tuscany and Umbria are particularly prized (and the most expensive).

The olive yield per tree from a quality grove in Tuscany, for example, is 10 kg (20 lb) which will give about 1 litre (1¾ pt) of Extra Virgin Olive Oil. Compare this to the average yield of 2.5-3 litres (4-5 pt) of oil per tree and you can see why there is such a variation in price. When choosing an oil, be guided by the price as well as the labelling. Some makers are beginning to state the olive variety on the label as well, for example frantoio is one of the main olives used in Tuscany for quality oil.

❖

PESTO

This traditional Italian sauce made with garlic, olive oil and basil is marvellous to have on hand to pep up vegetable soups, sauces, or just to toss through hot vegetables or pasta. Pesto can be stored in the refrigerator for up to two weeks.

Makes 125 mL (4 fl oz)

☐ **90 g (3 oz) fresh basil leaves**
☐ **3 cloves garlic, peeled**
☐ **2 tablespoons pine nuts**
☐ **125 mL (4 fl oz) olive oil**
☐ **4 tablespoons grated fresh Parmesan cheese**
☐ **freshly ground black pepper**

1 Place basil, garlic, pine nuts and 3 tablespoons olive oil in a food processor or blender and process until well combined. With machine running, gradually add remaining oil.

2 Transfer pesto to a bowl and mix in Parmesan cheese. Season to taste with pepper. Cover and refrigerate until required.

Vinegar
Vinegar used in Italian cooking is always wine vinegar. Wine vinegar is produced by the acetic fermentation of red or white wine. Malt and distilled vinegar are uncommon in Italy and are never used in cooking. The three most common vinegars are red wine vinegar, white wine vinegar and balsamic vinegar.

Balsamic vinegar is a dark red wine vinegar. It is made by the special processing of wines and musts from the Modena province. Balsamic vinegar is aged for between three and twelve years and the best is so sweet that it is used like a cordial and sprinkled over fresh berries or sipped after a rich meal. (See the recipe on page 75 for Strawberries in Balsamic Vinegar). It is an interesting addition to any salad dressing and can also be used in sauces for meats or vegetables. The best balsamic vinegar is very expensive.

❖

GARLIC VINEGAR

Use this in marinades, vinaigrettes or mayonnaise to give a subtle garlic flavour. Sprinkle olive oil and garlic vinegar over hot vegetables or pasta, toss and serve.

Makes 1 litre (1¾ pt)

☐ **1 head garlic, divided into cloves and crushed**
☐ **1 litre (1¾ pt) white wine vinegar**

Combine garlic and vinegar. Pour into a sterilised bottle and seal. Leave in a warm place for approximately one month. A sunny kitchen windowsill is ideal. Shake the bottle regularly. Strain, rebottle and label.

COOKING WITH OLIVE OIL

✧ Olive oil is used as a condiment as well as in cooking. It is as a dressing that Extra Virgin Olive Oil comes into its own.

✧ Olive oil can be used instead of butter in cooking. A mixture of butter and olive oil reduces splattering and the tendency of butter to burn.

✧ Olive oil contains no cholesterol and is highly digestible as its fats are completely absorbed by the body.

✧ It should be stored in tin, clay, stainless steel or tinted glass and kept in a cool, dark spot, not refrigerated. If affected by heat or light, it oxidises, changes to a brassy colour and turns rancid.

PIZZAS
and
BREADS

Keep your doors and windows shut when you cook these breads and pizzas or you may be bowled over in the neighbourhood rush! The aroma is sensational.

PIZZA DOUGH

Pizzas are easy and very satisfying to make at home. There is no secret to success; a well-kneaded dough and a light topping of complementary ingredients are all it takes. Apart from experimenting with a variety of flavours, try different shapes as well. Pizzas do not have to be large and round. Some are rectangles, some oval, some small individual circles called pizzette and some have a deep crust and sides more resembling a pie (which, after all, is what pizza means in Italian). The Basic Pizza Dough can be prepared several days ahead and set aside to rise before being knocked down, covered with plastic food wrap and refrigerated. Bring to room temperature 2-3 hours before shaping and second rising.

❖
BASIC PIZZA DOUGH

Dough for a 38-40 cm (15-16 in) pizza

- ☐ **1³/₄ teaspoons active dry yeast, or 15 g (¹/₂ oz) fresh yeast, crumbled**
- ☐ **pinch sugar**
- ☐ **335 mL (10¹/₂ fl oz) warm water**
- ☐ **125 mL (4 fl oz) olive oil**
- ☐ **500 g (1 lb) plain flour, sifted**
- ☐ **1¹/₄ teaspoons salt**

1   Dissolve yeast and sugar in water in a large mixing bowl. Set aside in a draught-free place for 5 minutes or until foamy. Stir in oil, flour and salt and mix until a rough dough forms. Turn out onto a lightly floured surface and knead for 5 minutes or until soft and satiny. Add more flour if necessary.
2   Lightly oil a large bowl then roll dough around in it to cover surface with oil. Seal bowl with plastic food wrap and place in a warm, draught-free spot for 1¹/₂-2 hours or until dough has doubled in volume.
3   Knock down and remove dough from bowl. Knead briefly before rolling out on a floured surface to desired shape. If dough feels too stiff, set aside to rest for a few minutes and start again.

4   Transfer to an oiled pizza pan and finish shaping by hand, forming a slightly raised rim. The dough should be approximately 5 mm (¹/₄ in) thick. For a thicker crust, cover with a clean tea-towel and set aside, for 30 minutes to rise again. The pizza is now ready for topping and baking.

To make in a food processor
Dissolve yeast and sugar in water in a small bowl. Set aside for 5 minutes or until foamy. Put flour and salt in food processor and pulse once or twice to sift. With machine running, slowly pour in yeast mixture and process for 10-15 seconds longer. Transfer to a lightly floured surface and knead by hand for 3-4 minutes. Continue as for basic recipe.

❖
QUICK PIZZA DOUGH

This dough takes very little time to make, is easy to handle, and can be made in advance and stored in the refrigerator. If some of the oil separates during storage, knead the dough to incorporate the oil again before using. Based on olive oil, white wine and sugar, the flavour is similar to a yeast dough but the uses are even more varied than the traditional pizza base.

Makes about 1 kg (2 lb) dough, or enough for 1 x 38-40 cm (15-16 in) pizza

- ☐ **540 g (17 oz) plain flour, sifted**
- ☐ **45 g (1¹/₂ oz) caster sugar**
- ☐ **1 teaspoon salt**
- ☐ **2 eggs, lightly beaten**
- ☐ **250 mL (8 fl oz) olive oil**
- ☐ **100 mL (3¹/₂ fl oz) dry white wine**

1   Mix flour, sugar and salt in a bowl. Gradually mix in eggs, oil and wine, beating well after each addition.
2   When a loose dough forms, transfer to a floured board and knead for 2-3

minutes or until smooth and satiny. Cover and refrigerate until required. Bring dough to room temperature before rolling out and using.

To make in a food processor

Place flour, sugar and salt in bowl and pulse once or twice to blend. With machine running, add eggs, then slowly pour in oil and wine. Continue until a smooth, glossy ball forms. Remove from processor and knead briefly. Cover and chill for 30 minutes before using.

❖

FOCACCIA DOUGH

Dough for 1 focaccia 28 x 38 cm (11 x 15 in), or 33 cm (13 in) round

- ☐ **1¼ teaspoons active dry yeast**
- ☐ **1 teaspoon sugar**
- ☐ **315 mL (9½ fl oz) lukewarm water**
- ☐ **1 tablespoon olive oil**
- ☐ **500 g (1 lb) plain flour, sifted**

1   Place yeast and sugar in a large bowl and stir in all but 1 tablespoon water. Cover and set aside in a warm place for 8-10 minutes or until foaming.

2   Stir in remaining water and oil. Add one-third flour and stir until smooth. Stir in the next one-third flour, beat, then add remaining flour. Mix until a rough dough forms. Transfer to a floured board and knead for 8-10 minutes, or until dough is smooth and satiny.

3   Place dough in a lightly oiled bowl, roll around to coat dough with oil. Cover bowl tightly with plastic food wrap. Set aside in a warm, draught-free spot for 1½ hours or until doubled in size.

4   Knock dough down, knead once or twice, then roll to desired shape. Place on an oiled oven tray, brush surface with a little oil, cover with a clean tea-towel and set aside to rise for 30 minutes longer.

5   Using your fingertips, dimple entire surface of dough, pushing in about halfway. Traditionally this serves to create little pools for the olive oil, but it also kneads the dough one last time. Re-cover with tea-towel and set aside again to rise for 1½-2 hours or until doubled. The focaccia is now ready for dressing and baking.

To make in a food processor

In a small bowl, stir yeast and sugar into warm water, cover and set aside in a warm place for 8-10 minutes or until foamy. Put flour and salt in processor bowl and pulse 2 or 3 times to mix. With machine running, pour in additional water, yeast and oil. Process until a rough dough forms, then continue to process to knead dough into a firm ball. Transfer to a floured board and knead by hand for 2-3 minutes.

FOCACCIA

Focaccia, a large, flat oval or rectangle of bread, turns up all over Italy in a number of guises and with just as many names! Around Florence it is known as schiacciata, but this can mean small individual focaccia in other areas. In its simplest form it is flavoured with olive oil, salt, and garlic or herbs, then sliced and filled much the same as a sandwich. It can be topped with any variety of ingredients, or filled before baking. There can be thick, soft ones and thin, crisp ones. Whatever its presentation, focaccia is a true product of its rustic origins.

Getting to know yeast

There are two types of yeast that are commonly used in breadmaking – fresh and dried.

✧   Dried yeast works as well as fresh but takes longer to activate. As it is twice as concentrated as fresh yeast only half as much is needed. You will find that 15 g (½ oz) dried yeast has the same raising power as 30 g (1 oz) fresh yeast.

✧   Fresh yeast will keep in a loosely tied polythene bag in the refrigerator for about a week.

✧   Dried yeast will keep in a cool dark place for about six months. Yeast will deteriorate if exposed to air.

✧   Yeast works best in warm conditions. Cold and draughts slow down its growth, whereas an intense heat will kill it.

✧   The amount of yeast required depends on the richness of the dough. The more sugar and fat there is in a dough, the more yeast it needs to make it rise.

✧   Using too much yeast will give a crumbly, sour-tasting bread which will go stale quickly.

✧   Fresh yeast works best when mixed with liquid that is at about 25°C (78°F) and dried yeast at 40°C (104°F).

✧   An easy way of making sure that the liquid is at the right temperature is to bring one-third of it to the boil and add the rest cold.

CHICKEN AND ASPARAGUS CALZONE

A calzone is basically a pizza folded over to encase the filling. Because the filling is sealed in during baking it is much more succulent.

Makes 1 large calzone

- ☐ ½ recipe Basic Pizza Dough (page 46)
- ☐ 1 large zucchini (courgette), sliced
- ☐ salt
- ☐ 200 g (6½ oz) fresh asparagus spears, trimmed, blanched and cut into 5 cm (2 in) pieces
- ☐ 250 g (8 oz) cooked chicken meat, cut into 2.5 cm (1 in) pieces
- ☐ 30 g (1 oz) ham, diced
- ☐ 100 g (3½ oz) ricotta cheese, drained
- ☐ 1 tablespoon grated fresh Parmesan cheese
- ☐ freshly ground black pepper
- ☐ olive oil

1   Prepare Basic Pizza Dough as described in recipe.
2   Sprinkle zucchini (courgette) with salt, place in sieve and drain for 20 minutes. Rinse and pat dry with absorbent kitchen paper.
3   Combine zucchini (courgette), asparagus, chicken, ham, ricotta cheese and Parmesan cheese. Season to taste with black pepper, and stir in a little olive oil.
4   Roll out dough to 5 mm (¼ in) thick circle, about 30 cm (12 in) diameter. Pile filling onto one half. Fold uncovered side over filling, folding edges up and in to seal. Crimp or flute to neaten.
5   Transfer to an oiled baking tray, brush with olive oil and bake at 200°C (400°F/Gas 6) for 20-25 minutes.until golden brown. Stand for 5-10 minutes before serving.

❖

RICOTTA FOCACCIA

A layer of ricotta sandwiched in the middle of focaccia gives a soft, moist variation which is as good served as an accompaniment to a meal, or as a mid-day snack.

Makes 1 loaf

- ☐ 1 recipe Focaccia Dough (page 47)
- ☐ 250 g (8 oz) ricotta cheese, drained in cheesecloth for 2 hours
- ☐ 1 tablespoon chopped fresh basil
- ☐ 3 tablespoons olive oil
- ☐ 1 tablespoon coarse sea salt

1   Prepare Focaccia Dough, as described in recipe through to the end of step 3. Knock down dough and knead briefly. Divide mixture into two portions and roll each out to a thin circle about 33 cm (13 in) diameter.
2   Transfer one circle to a greased baking tray, and spread evenly with ricotta. Sprinkle with basil. Cover with the second dough circle and seal edges together. Dimple surface with fingertips, brush with 1 tablespoon oil, cover with a clean tea-towel and set aside to rise for 1-2 hours or until doubled.
3   Brush surface with remaining olive oil and sprinkle with salt. Bake at 200°C (400°F/Gas 6) for 20-25 minutes or until golden. Remove from oven and invert onto wire racks to cool. Serve warm.

❖

CHEESE AND BACON PANZEROTTI

These little turnovers are usually eaten for lunch or supper. If made smaller they are perfect as finger food. Any naturally smoked cheese can be used.

Makes 20-25

- ☐ 1 recipe Quick Pizza Dough (page 46)

FILLING
- ☐ 500 g (1 lb) ricotta cheese, drained
- ☐ 3 eggs, lightly beaten
- ☐ 200 g (6½ oz) smoked mozzarella cheese, finely diced
- ☐ 155 g (5 oz) bacon rashers, trimmed of fat and finely diced
- ☐ 1½ tablespoons grated fresh Parmesan cheese
- ☐ ½ teaspoon freshly ground black pepper
- ☐ 3½ tablespoons breadcrumbs, made from stale bread
- ☐ 2 tablespoons finely chopped fresh mint

1   Prepare Quick Pizza Dough as described in recipe. Divide dough into two equal portions. Roll out each portion on a floured board to 3 mm (⅛ in) thickness. Cut into rounds, using a 10-13 cm (4-5 in) cutter.
2   To make filling, combine ricotta cheese, half egg mixture, mozzarella cheese, bacon, Parmesan cheese, black pepper, breadcrumbs and mint in a bowl.
4   Place a heaped tablespoon in centre of each dough round. Brush edges with some of remaining egg, then fold sides together to form a half circle or crescent. Press sides together well and go around cut edge with either a crimper-cutter or a fork pattern. Brush surface with egg and transfer panzerotti to a greased oven tray. Bake at 180°C (350°F/Gas 4) for 12-15 minutes or until puffed and golden.

Ricotta Focaccia, Cheese and Bacon Panzerotti, Chicken and Asparagus Calzone

Tiles Country Floors Urn and Column Parterre Garden Glasses Glebe Hot Glass Studio

GRISSINI WITH FENNEL SEEDS

Grissini are easy to make with leftover pizza dough. If you are going to start from scratch, substitute 1 tablespoon malt syrup for the sugar in the Basic Pizza Dough recipe.

For 20-25 sticks

- ☐ **1 recipe Basic Pizza Dough (page 46)**
- ☐ **4 tablespoons coarse salt**
- ☐ **2 tablespoons fennel seeds**

1 Prepare Basic Pizza Dough as described in recipe, to end of Step 2. Knock down, remove from bowl and knead briefly.

2 Cut dough into four equal portions. Shape each portion into a rectangle 1 cm (¹/₂ in) thick. Sprinkle each portion with salt and fennel seeds. Cut each piece into 5-6 uniform strips about 1 cm (¹/₂ in) thick.

3 Transfer each strip to a lightly oiled baking tray, stretching strips to desired length. Place 4-5 cm (1¹/₂-2 in) apart on tray and bake at 200°C (400°F/Gas 6) for 15 minutes or until golden. Cool on wire racks then store in an airtight container.

ROSEMARY AND GARLIC WHOLEMEAL SCHIACCIATA

Small, individual focaccia which are great to munch on any time of the day.

Makes 3 schiacciate

- ☐ **1 recipe Focaccia Dough, (page 47), substitute 125 g (4 oz) plain flour with 125 g (4 oz) wholemeal plain flour**
- ☐ **4 cloves garlic, crushed**
- ☐ **3-4 tablespoons olive oil**
- ☐ **2 tablespoons chopped fresh rosemary**
- ☐ **1 tablespoon coarse salt**

1 Prepare Focaccia Dough, as described in recipe, to the end of Step 3.

2 Knock down dough and knead lightly. Divide into three portions and shape into balls. Roll out each ball on a lightly floured board to a circle 5 mm (¹/₄ in) thick. Transfer to oiled baking trays, brush with a little oil and cover with clean tea-towels. Set aside to rise in a warm, draught-free place for 45 minutes or until puffy.

3 Heat garlic and olive oil together in a small saucepan for 7-8 minutes. Remove from heat and set aside to cool for 30 minutes. Remove and discard garlic.

4 Dimple surface of each bread, using fingertips. Brush with oil and sprinkle with rosemary and salt.

5 Bake at 200°C (400°F/Gas 6) for 15-20 minutes, or until golden. Stand on trays for 5 minutes before serving, or transfer to wire racks to cool. Eat at room temperature.

FRIED FLATBREAD

Using Quick Pizza Dough, Fried Flatbread is perfect as a snack, an accompaniment to soup or to nibble on over a glass of vino.

Makes 12-15

- ☐ **ingredients for 1 recipe Quick Pizza Dough (page 46)**
- ☐ **1 small red pepper, finely chopped**
- ☐ **1 small onion, finely chopped**
- ☐ **12 pitted black olives, finely chopped**
- ☐ **2 cloves garlic, crushed (optional)**
- ☐ **vegetable oil for cooking**

1 Make up Quick Pizza Dough as described in recipe. Add red pepper, onion and olives with dry ingredients. Knead and set aside to rest for 1¹/₂ hours.

2 Divide dough into 18 portions and using floured hands, roll each into a firm ball. On a lightly floured board, roll out each ball to form a circle 3 mm (¹/₈ in) thick. Sprinkle garlic onto one side of each bread and roll lightly.

3 Heat 1 tablespoon vegetable oil in a frypan, and cook bread rounds, one at a time, until edges are golden and beginning to bubble. Turn once during cooking. Add more oil if necessary. Remove from pan, drain on absorbent kitchen paper and cool on a wire rack. Store in an airtight container for up to 1 week.

Jug Hale Imports *Floor Ware* Collingwood Floors *Glasses* Glebe Hot Glass Studio

GARLIC FOCACCIA

A basic, but very special bread which looks great and imparts the rustic flavours of olive oil and garlic.

Makes 1 loaf

- ☐ **1 recipe Focaccia Dough (page 47)**
- ☐ **3 tablespoons olive oil**
- ☐ **4 cloves garlic, crushed**
- ☐ **1 tablespoon coarse sea salt**

1   Make up Focaccia Dough as described in recipe to end of Step 4.
2   Combine olive oil with garlic and brush over dough. Sprinkle with salt and bake at 200°C (400°F/Gas 6) for 20-25 minutes or until golden. Remove from oven and invert onto a wire rack to cool.

Variations:

Raisin and Fresh Sage: Top focaccia with 3 tablespoons olive oil, 4 tablespoons raisins soaked in Marsala for 30 minutes, and 1 heaped tablespoon chopped fresh sage.

Olives and Pancetta: Top focaccia with 3 tablespoons olive oil, 125 g (4 oz) black olives and 100 g (3½ oz) diced pancetta.

SPINACH, OLIVE AND ONION BREAD

A filled bread, almost a pie, this flat loaf makes a delicious snack or supper dish.

Serves 8

- ☐ **1 recipe Focaccia Dough, (page 47)**
- ☐ **1 tablespoon olive oil**
- ☐ **1 egg white, lightly beaten**

FILLING

- ☐ **2 tablespoons olive oil**
- ☐ **1 large red onion, sliced**
- ☐ **1 clove garlic, crushed**
- ☐ **1 tablespoon sultanas**
- ☐ **750 g (1½ lb) spinach, stalks removed and leaves shredded**
- ☐ **125 g (4 oz) stuffed green olives, sliced**
- ☐ **3 tablespoons grated fresh mozzarella cheese**
- ☐ **freshly ground black pepper**

1   Prepare Focaccia Dough, as described in recipe through to end of Step 3.
2   To make filling, heat olive oil in a large frypan and cook onion until soft. Add garlic and sultanas and cook 1 minute longer. Add spinach and olives and cook over a medium heat until spinach just begins to wilt. Remove from heat and mix in mozzarella. Season to taste with black pepper. Set aside.
3   Knock down dough and knead lightly. Divide dough into four portions, and roll out into circles 5 mm (¼ in) thick. Place two circles on lightly oiled baking trays, then spread with filling to within 2.5 cm (1 in) of edge. Cover with remaining circles and pinch sides together to seal edges.
4   Brush top with olive oil. Cover with a clean tea-towel and set aside to rise in a warm place until doubled in size.
5   Brush top with egg white and bake at 200°C (400°F/Gas 6) for 25 minutes, or until golden brown and well risen.

From left: Grissini with Fennel Seeds, Rosemary and Garlic Wholemeal Schiacciata, Fried Flatbread, Garlic Focaccia, Spinach, Olive and Onion Bread

DEEP-SIDED PIZZA WITH TUNA, OLIVES, ANCHOVIES AND TOMATOES

A cross between a pizza and a pie, deep-sided pizzas are quite filling, so are more often served as a main meal. This version, typical of the Mediterranean with seafood, olives and tomatoes, makes a wonderful lunch. Use a 25 cm (10 in) round tin with 5-6 cm (2-2¹/₂ in) sides.

Serves 4-6

- ☐ ¹/₂ recipe Basic Pizza Dough (page 46)
- ☐ olive oil
- ☐ 440 g (14 oz) canned tuna, drained, broken up into chunks
- ☐ lemon juice
- ☐ freshly ground black pepper
- ☐ 400 g (12¹/₂ oz) grated fresh mozzarella cheese
- ☐ 4 tablespoons grated fresh Parmesan cheese
- ☐ 2 tablespoons chopped fresh parsley
- ☐ 60 g (2 oz) pitted black olives
- ☐ 10 whole anchovy fillets, drained and halved lengthways

SAUCE
- ☐ 2 tablespoons olive oil
- ☐ 1 large red onion, cut into slices, lengthways
- ☐ 1 large green pepper, sliced
- ☐ 1 clove garlic, crushed
- ☐ 4 tomatoes, peeled, seeded and chopped
- ☐ ¹/₂ teaspoon sugar
- ☐ 1 tablespoon minced anchovy fillets
- ☐ freshly ground black pepper

1   Prepare Basic Pizza Dough as described in recipe. Brush a 33 cm (13 in) pizza tray with olive oil and line with dough, pressing dough up sides to form a 4 cm (1¹/₂ in) rim. Brush dough with olive oil and set aside.

2   To make sauce, heat oil in a large frypan and cook onion, green pepper and garlic for 6-8 minutes. Stir in tomatoes, sugar and anchovies. Season to taste with black pepper.

3   To assemble, combine tuna, lemon juice and black pepper to taste. Combine one-third mozzarella with 1 tablespoon Parmesan cheese and sprinkle over pizza base. Top with half tuna mixture, sprinkle with 1 tablespoon parsley and 30 g (1 oz) olives. Spoon half the sauce mixture over. Repeat layers, finishing with a layer of mozzarella and Parmesan cheese.

4   Fold excess dough back on itself and crimp edges neatly. Arrange anchovies, in a diamond pattern on top of pizza. Halve remaining olives and place one in centre of each diamond. Drizzle over some olive oil and bake at 220°C (425°F/Gas7) for 15-20 minutes or until golden.

❖

GORGONZOLA AND SAGE PIZZA

This is as good straight from the oven as it is cooled and taken on a picnic. Allowing the dough to rise for 30 minutes before topping will give a thicker, more bread-like crust.

Makes 1 pizza 30-33 cm (12-13 in) round

- ☐ ¹/₂ recipe Basic Pizza Dough, or ¹/₂ recipe Quick Pizza Dough (page 46)
- ☐ 1 large eggplant (aubergine), cut into 5 mm (¹/₄ in) slices
- ☐ salt
- ☐ 220 mL (7 fl oz) olive oil
- ☐ 155 g (5 oz) Gorgonzola cheese
- ☐ 400 g (12¹/₂ oz) ricotta cheese, drained
- ☐ 1 teaspoon finely chopped fresh sage, or ¹/₄ teaspoon dried sage
- ☐ 3 tablespoons pine nuts
- ☐ 3 tablespoons grated fresh Parmesan cheese
- ☐ freshly ground black pepper
- ☐ sage leaves for garnish

1   Prepare Basic Pizza Dough or Quick Pizza Dough as described in recipes.

2   Place eggplant (aubergine) slices in colander, sprinkle with salt and set aside to drain for 30 minutes. Rinse under cold running water and pat dry with absorbent kitchen paper. Heat 125 mL (4 fl oz) olive oil in a large frypan and cook eggplant (aubergine), a few slices at a time, until lightly golden on both sides. Drain on absorbent kitchen paper.

3   Shape dough into a circle about 38 cm (15 in) round and 5 mm (¹/₄ in) thick for Basic Pizza Dough, and 1 cm (¹/₂ in) thick for Quick Pizza Dough and place on a baking tray. Bring up sides to form a slight rim. Brush with olive oil. Combine Gorgonzola and ricotta cheeses and spread evenly over dough. Arrange eggplant (aubergine) slices over top. Sprinkle with sage, pine nuts, Parmesan cheese and black pepper to taste, then drizzle on a little olive oil.

4   Garnish with sage leaves. Bake at 220°C (425°F/Gas 7) for 15 minutes. Reduce heat to 190°C (375°F/Gas 5) and bake for 10 minutes longer.

❖

ARTICHOKE, MOZZARELLA AND SALAMI PIZZA

Not all pizzas need a layer of tomato sauce to give them flavour and keep them moist. This tasty combination of toppings is a delicious and striking example.

Makes 1 pizza

- ☐ ¹/₂ recipe Basic Pizza Dough, or ¹/₂ recipe Quick Pizza Dough (page 46)
- ☐ olive oil
- ☐ 300 g (9¹/₂ oz) thinly sliced fresh mozzarella
- ☐ 100 g (3¹/₂ oz) thinly sliced Milano salami
- ☐ 4 canned artichoke hearts, thinly sliced, lengthways
- ☐ freshly ground black pepper

1   Roll dough into rectangle 1 cm (¹/₂ in) thick and press into a lightly oiled shallow 28 x 18 cm (11 x 7 in) tin and bring dough up at edges to form a slight rim. Brush with olive oil.

2   Place slices of mozzarella, slices of salami and slices of artichoke heart slightly overlapping in lines along width of dough. Continue forming rows of mozzarella, salami and artichoke heart until surface is covered. Sprinkle generously with olive oil, and season to taste with black pepper.

3   Bake at 220°C (425°F/Gas 7) for 15 minutes, then reduce heat to 190°C (375°F/Gas 5) and bake for 10 minutes longer or until cheese is bubbling and crust golden brown. Remove from oven and rest briefly before serving.

Deep-Sided Pizza with Tuna, Olives, Anchovies and Tomatoes, Artichoke, Mozzarella and Salami Pizza, Gorgonzola and Sage Pizza

Coffee Service Zyliss Plaque Patterre Garden

MEAT, GAME
and
POULTRY

Luxurious slow baking, intriguing stuffings and the use of unusual cuts characterise the cooking of most meats in Italy. Learn the secrets.

VEAL WITH WHITE WINE

Serves 4

- [ ] **4 veal chops, trimmed of all visible fat**
- [ ] **seasoned flour**
- [ ] **30 g (1 oz) butter**
- [ ] **1 clove garlic, crushed**
- [ ] **2 bacon rashers, chopped**
- [ ] **2 tablespoons chopped fresh rosemary**
- [ ] **250 mL (8 fl oz) dry white wine**

1   Coat chops in flour and set aside. Melt butter in a frypan and cook garlic, bacon and rosemary for 1 minute. Add chops and brown on both sides.

2   Stir in wine, bring to the boil, reduce heat, cover pan and simmer gently for 30 minutes or until veal is cooked.

3   Remove veal and set aside to keep warm. Increase heat and bring wine to the boil. Boil until reduced and a glaze forms.

FRESH BASIL CARPACCIO

To achieve very thin slices, wrap the fillet in plastic food wrap and place in the freezer for 15 minutes or until firm, then slice with a very sharp knife.

Serves 4

- [ ] **500 g (1 lb) eye fillet in one piece, very thinly sliced**
- [ ] **freshly ground black pepper**
- [ ] **1 onion, finely sliced**

BASIL DRESSING
- [ ] **10 fresh basil leaves, chopped**
- [ ] **4 tablespoons olive oil**
- [ ] **3 tablespoons lemon juice**
- [ ] **2 tablespoons capers, chopped**
- [ ] **2 cloves garlic, finely chopped**

1   To make dressing, place basil, oil, lemon juice, capers and garlic in a bowl. Mix well to combine.

2   Arrange beef slices on a serving plate and season with black pepper. Pour dressing over and sprinkle with onion. Cover and marinate for 10 minutes.

PIGEON WITH RED WINE

Serves 4

- [ ] **4 pigeons**
- [ ] **2 tablespoons olive oil**
- [ ] **2 tablespoons grated lemon rind**
- [ ] **2 tablespoons chopped fresh parsley**
- [ ] **4 sage leaves, chopped**
- [ ] **2 cloves garlic, crushed**
- [ ] **2 tablespoons capers, chopped**
- [ ] **6 anchovy fillets, chopped**
- [ ] **250 mL (8 fl oz) dry red wine**
- [ ] **freshly ground black pepper**

1   Section pigeons, leaving breast fillets whole.

2   Heat oil in a frypan and cook pigeon and lemon rind for 3-4 minutes each side or until brown. Add parsley, sage, garlic, capers and anchovies and cook, stirring, for 2 minutes.

3   Stir in wine, bring to the boil and simmer covered for 1 hour or until pigeon is tender. Season with black pepper.

Pigeon with Red Wine, Fresh Basil Carpaccio, Veal with White Wine

*Plates Mikasa Floor Ware Collingwood Floors
Glass and Urn Glebe Hot Glass Studio
Etching Phillips & Company Gallery*

DUCK WITH BALSAMIC VINEGAR

Blueberries are used in this recipe, but any other berry fruit may be substituted.

Serves 4

- ☐ 2 tablespoons sunflower oil
- ☐ 4 duck breasts
- ☐ 3 tablespoons balsamic vinegar
- ☐ freshly ground black pepper
- ☐ ¹/₄ teaspoon ground cinnamon
- ☐ 4 tablespoons fresh blueberries

ZUCCHINI (COURGETTE) FLOWERS
- ☐ 90 g (3 oz) flour
- ☐ 250 mL (8 fl oz) water
- ☐ oil for cooking
- ☐ 12 zucchini (courgette) flowers

1   Heat oil in a frypan and cook duck, skin side down, over a low heat until skin is golden. Turn and cook other side.

2   Add vinegar, black pepper to taste, cinnamon and blueberries. Cover and cook over a low heat for 15 minutes, or until duck is tender.

3   To prepare flowers, gradually sift flour into water and mix with a fork until batter is smooth. If necessary add more water. Pour 2.5 cm (1 in) oil into a frypan and heat until very hot. Dip flowers into the batter and cook a few at a time in oil until golden.

4   To serve, arrange duck and flowers on serving plate and spoon blueberry sauce over duck.

❖

CHICKEN MARSALA

Serves 4

- ☐ 4 large chicken breast fillets, pounded
- ☐ seasoned flour
- ☐ 30 g (1 oz) butter
- ☐ 2 tablespoons olive oil
- ☐ 185 mL (6 fl oz) dry Marsala
- ☐ 4 tablespoons chicken stock
- ☐ 30 g (1 oz) butter, softened
- ☐ freshly ground black pepper

1   Coat chicken in flour and shake off excess. Heat butter and oil in a frypan, until butter is foaming. Add chicken and cook for 3 minutes each side.

2   Stir in Marsala, bring to the boil and simmer for 15 minutes, or until chicken is cooked. Remove chicken and set aside to keep warm. Add stock, bring to the boil and boil for 2 minutes. Whisk in softened butter and season to taste with black pepper. To serve, spoon sauce over chicken.

❖

QUAIL WITH RICE AND OLIVES

Serves 4

- [ ] **1 tablespoon olive oil**
- [ ] **30 g (1 oz) butter**
- [ ] **2 onions, chopped**
- [ ] **2 cloves garlic, crushed**
- [ ] **8 quail, cleaned**
- [ ] **5 fresh sage leaves**
- [ ] **3 teaspoons chopped fresh rosemary**
- [ ] **freshly ground black pepper**
- [ ] **300 mL (9½ fl oz) dry Marsala**

OLIVE RICE
- [ ] **375 g (12 oz) rice, cooked**
- [ ] **60 g (2 oz) butter, chopped**
- [ ] **6 slices mortadella, chopped**
- [ ] **90 g (3 oz) pitted black olives, chopped**
- [ ] **3 tablespoons grated fresh Parmesan cheese**
- [ ] **3 tablespoons chopped fresh basil**

1 Heat oil and butter in a frypan and cook onions and garlic over a low heat for 3 minutes, or until onions soften.
2 Add quail to pan and cook over a high heat until brown on all sides. Add sage, rosemary and black pepper to taste.
3 Stir in Marsala, bring to the boil and simmer for 20 minutes or until quail is cooked.
4 To prepare rice, place rice, butter, mortadella and olives in a saucepan and heat gently, stirring, until butter is melted. Mix in Parmesan cheese and basil. To serve, arrange rice on serving plate, top with quail and spoon a little of the pan juices over.

Quail with Rice and Olives, Duck with Balsamic Vinegar, Chicken Marsala

Bowl Interim *Plates* Villeroy & Boch *Fabrics* Boyac Decorative Fabrics *Cutlery* Bibelot *Background* Ware Collingwood Floors *Bust and Glass* Corso de Fiori

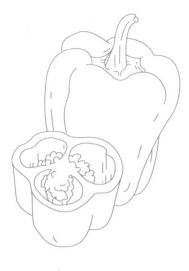

LAMB WITH EGG SAUCE

It is important when making this recipe that you do not allow the lamb to boil after adding the egg yolks. This dish is wonderful served with fried eggplant (aubergine) and roasted peppers.

Serves 8

- ☐ **1 kg (2 lb) cubed lamb**
- ☐ **3 tablespoons lemon juice**
- ☐ **2 tablespoons olive oil**
- ☐ **30 g (1 oz) butter**
- ☐ **1 onion, sliced**
- ☐ **4 slices ham, chopped**
- ☐ **1 tablespoon plain flour**
- ☐ **250 mL (8 fl oz) dry white wine**
- ☐ **60 mL (2 fl oz) beef stock**
- ☐ **1 tablespoon grated lemon rind**
- ☐ **3 egg yolks, lightly beaten**
- ☐ **2 tablespoons chopped fresh parsley**
- ☐ **1 tablespoon chopped fresh marjoram**

1   Combine lamb and 1 tablespoon lemon juice in a bowl. Toss to combine and set aside for 30 minutes. Drain lamb and pat dry on absorbent kitchen paper. Heat oil and butter in a frypan and cook onion until soft. Add ham and lamb to onions and cook for 4-5 minutes.

2   Add flour and cook, stirring, until lamb is coated. Stir in wine and stock. Bring to the boil, then reduce heat, cover and cook over a low heat for 30 minutes or until lamb is tender.

3   Add lemon rind and remaining lemon juice and cook for 3 minutes longer. Stir in egg yolks and cook, without boiling, for 3-4 minutes or until heated through. Remove from heat and mix in parsley and marjoram.

❖

RABBIT-FILLED PEPPERS

Serves 4

- ☐ **4 red or green peppers**
- ☐ **60 g (2 oz) butter**
- ☐ **750 g (1½ lb) rabbit, boned and flesh finely chopped**
- ☐ **2 onions, chopped**
- ☐ **125 g (4 oz) mushrooms, chopped**
- ☐ **3 spinach leaves, stalks removed and leaves chopped**
- ☐ **125 mL (4 fl oz) dry white wine**
- ☐ **125 mL (4 fl oz) chicken stock**
- ☐ **1 tablespoon concentrated tomato paste**
- ☐ **freshly ground black pepper**
- ☐ **2 tablespoons chopped fresh parsley**
- ☐ **3 teaspoons chopped fresh rosemary**

1   Cut a 2.5 cm (1 in) slice from top of each pepper and set aside. Scrape seeds from peppers. Place pepper shells on a baking tray and bake at 180°C (350°F/ Gas 4) for 20 minutes, or until shells are tender but still holding their shape.

2   Melt butter in a frypan and cook rabbit and onions for 5 minutes or until lightly browned. Add mushrooms and spinach and cook, stirring, for 1 minute longer. Stir in wine and bring to the boil and cook until reduced by half. Add stock, tomato paste and black pepper to taste, bring to the boil and simmer for 15 minutes. Stir in parsley and rosemary.

3   Fill pepper shells with rabbit mixture, top with lids and bake at 180°C (350°F/ Gas 4) for 15 minutes.

❖

BEEF POT ROAST

Polenta makes a great accompaniment to this traditional dish.

Serves 4

- ☐ **1.5 kg (3 lb) piece topside beef**
- ☐ **60 g (2 oz) butter**
- ☐ **1 onion, chopped**
- ☐ **250 mL (8 fl oz) dry white wine**

MARINADE
- ☐ **2 cloves garlic, crushed**
- ☐ **2 whole cloves**
- ☐ **pinch ground cinnamon**
- ☐ **600 mL (1 pt) white wine vinegar**
- ☐ **2 stalks celery, chopped**
- ☐ **1 sprig fresh rosemary**
- ☐ **5 whole black peppercorns**

1   To make marinade, place garlic, cloves, cinnamon, vinegar, celery, rosemary and peppercorns in a bowl and mix well. Add beef and toss to coat. Cover and refrigerate for 12 hours or overnight. Remove beef and strain marinade. Reserve solids and discard liquid.

2   Melt butter in a large heavy-based saucepan, add meat and brown on all sides. Remove from pan and set aside.

3   Add onion and reserved solids to pan and cook over a low heat for 5 minutes or until onion softens. Return meat to pan. Pour in wine and bring to the boil, then reduce heat to low. Cover pan with a tightly fitting lid and cook for 2½ hours or until meat is very tender. Cut meat into slices and serve with any sauce that has formed during cooking.

❖

VEAL ESCALOPES

Serve this easy veal dish with a fresh green salad.

Serves 4

- ☐ **8 small, thin veal steaks**
- ☐ **seasoned flour**
- ☐ **1 egg, lightly beaten**
- ☐ **185 g (6 oz) breadcrumbs, made from stale bread**
- ☐ **60 g (2 oz) butter**
- ☐ **8 slices prosciutto**
- ☐ **125 g (4 oz) grated mozzarella cheese**
- ☐ **3 tablespoons grated fresh Parmesan cheese**
- ☐ **125 mL (4 fl oz) thickened cream (double)**

1   Place veal slices between plastic food wrap and flatten using a mallet, until very thin. Coat veal in flour, dip in egg then coat with breadcrumbs.

2   Melt butter in a frypan until foaming. Add veal and cook for 2 minutes each side or until golden. Wrap each veal steak in a slice of prosciutto, place in a shallow baking dish and sprinkle with mozzarella and Parmesan cheeses. Spoon cream over and cook under a preheated grill for 3-4 minutes, or until cheese melts and is golden.

Beef Pot Roast, Rabbit-Filled Peppers, Lamb with Egg Sauce, Veal Escalopes

Floor Ware Collingwood Floors *Fabric and Print* Made Where *Urn* Parterre Garden *Plate* J.D. Milner *Glass* Mikasa Tableware *Pot* Home and Garden *Salt and Pepper Shakers* Interim

SPATCHCOCK WITH RICOTTA AND HERBS

Serves 4

- [ ] **4 x 500 g (1 lb) spatchcocks, cleaned and dried**
- [ ] **2 tablespoons olive oil**
- [ ] **4 fresh rosemary sprigs**
- [ ] **freshly ground black pepper**
- [ ] **375 mL (12 fl oz) dry white wine**

STUFFING
- [ ] **155 g (5 oz) ricotta cheese**
- [ ] **60 g (2 oz) finely grated fontina cheese**
- [ ] **60 g (2 oz) Gorgonzola cheese, crumbled**
- [ ] **4 slices mortadella, finely chopped**
- [ ] **2 tablespoons chopped fresh parsley**
- [ ] **1 tablespoon chopped fresh marjoram**
- [ ] **1 tablespoon chopped fresh sage**
- [ ] **30 g (1 oz) butter, melted**

1   To make stuffing, place ricotta cheese, fontina cheese, Gorgonzola cheese, mortadella, parsley, marjoram, sage and butter in a bowl and mix well. Divide into four portions. Gently ease skin from breast of each bird and fill pocket with stuffing.

2   Brush birds with oil and top with a sprig of rosemary and a sprinkle of black pepper. Place on a roasting rack in a baking dish and cook at 220°C (425°F/Gas 7) for 30 minutes. Reduce heat to 180°C (350°F/Gas 4) and cook, basting with pan juices, for 20 minutes longer or until birds are tender.

3   Remove birds and set aside to keep warm. Place baking dish over a hot plate and bring juices to the boil, pour over birds and serve.

❖

OSSO BUCCO

The name of this recipe means 'hollow bones' and is a specialty from Milan.

Serves 4

- [ ] **30 g (1 oz) butter**
- [ ] **1 carrot, chopped**
- [ ] **2 onions, chopped**
- [ ] **2 stalks celery, chopped**
- [ ] **2 cloves garlic, crushed**
- [ ] **4 thick slices shin veal on the bone**
- [ ] **flour**
- [ ] **2 tablespoons olive oil**
- [ ] **8 tomatoes, peeled and chopped**
- [ ] **125 mL (4 fl oz) dry white wine**
- [ ] **250 mL (8 fl oz) beef stock**
- [ ] **1 bay leaf**
- [ ] **freshly ground black pepper**
- [ ] **1 tablespoon butter mixed with 2 tablespoons flour**

GREMOLATA
- [ ] **4 tablespoons chopped fresh parsley**
- [ ] **1 tablespoon finely grated lemon rind**
- [ ] **1 clove garlic, crushed**
- [ ] **1 anchovy, finely chopped**

1   Melt butter in a frypan and cook carrot, onions, celery and garlic gently for 5 minutes, or until vegetables are softened. Remove vegetables from pan and place in an ovenproof dish.

2   Coat veal in flour. Heat oil in a frypan and cook veal until golden on each side. Remove from pan and arrange over vegetables.

3   Add tomatoes and cook stirring constantly for 5 minutes. Blend in wine, stock, bay leaf and black pepper to taste, bring to the boil and simmer for 5 minutes. Whisk in butter mixture and pour over meat and vegetables.

4   Cover dish and bake at 180°C (350°F/Gas 4) for 1½ hours or until meat is tender.

5   To make Gremolata, combine parsley, lemon rind, garlic and anchovy. Sprinkle over meat just prior to serving.

Tiles Country Floors Dishes Hale Imports Painting The Bay House Studio

Plate J.D. Milner *Bowls* Phillips and Company Gallery *Column Made Where*

PARMESAN AND BASIL TRIPE

Serves 4

- ☐ **2 tablespoons olive oil**
- ☐ **1 onion, chopped**
- ☐ **1 carrot, chopped**
- ☐ **1 stalk celery, chopped**
- ☐ **1 clove garlic, crushed**
- ☐ **2 bay leaves**
- ☐ **1 sprig fresh rosemary**
- ☐ **6 tomatoes, peeled and chopped**
- ☐ **250 mL (8 fl oz) dry white wine**
- ☐ **1 kg (2 lb) tripe, cut into thin strips**
- ☐ **2 tablespoons chopped fresh basil**
- ☐ **3 tablespoons chopped fresh parsley**
- ☐ **4 tablespoons grated fresh Parmesan cheese**

1   Heat oil in a frypan and cook onion, carrot and celery over a low heat for 5 minutes, or until vegetables soften. Add garlic, bay leaves and rosemary and cook for 2 minutes longer.

2   Stir in tomatoes and wine, bring to the boil, then reduce heat and simmer until reduced by half. Add tripe and cook over a low heat for 1-1½ hours or until tripe is tender. Mix in basil, parsley, and Parmesan cheese and serve.

PORK BRAISED IN MILK

This dish originates from Bologna and is often preceded by dishes with a Bolognese sauce. Pork cooked this way goes well with artichokes.

Serves 4

- ☐ **30 g (1 oz) butter**
- ☐ **1 tablespoon vegetable oil**
- ☐ **1 kg (2 lb) boneless loin pork, rolled and tied**
- ☐ **500 mL (16 fl oz) milk**
- ☐ **freshly ground black pepper**
- ☐ **3 tablespoons warm water**

1   Heat butter and oil in a large saucepan. When butter is foaming, add pork and brown on all sides.

2   Add milk, and pepper to taste and bring to the boil. Reduce heat to low, cover and cook for 1½-2 hours or until pork is cooked. Brush pork occasionally with milk during cooking.

3   At end of cooking time, milk should have coagulated and browned in bottom of pan. If this has not occurred remove lid, and bring liquid to the boil and boil until brown.

4   Remove meat from pan and set aside to cool slightly. Remove string from pork, cut into slices and arrange on a serving platter. Set aside to keep warm.

5   Remove any fat from pan, stir in water and bring to the boil, scraping residue from base of the pan. Strain and spoon pan juices over pork to serve.

Above: Spatchcock with Ricotta and Herbs, Parmesan and Basil Tripe
Left: Pork Braised in Milk, Osso Bucco

LIVER WITH SAGE AND MUSHROOMS

Serves 4

- [ ] **30 g (1 oz) butter**
- [ ] **2 bacon rashers, chopped**
- [ ] **3 spring onions (shallots), chopped**
- [ ] **750 g (1½ lb) calves liver, skin removed and cut into strips**
- [ ] **8 fresh sage leaves**
- [ ] **125 mL (4 fl oz) dry white wine**
- [ ] **8 button mushrooms, halved**
- [ ] **freshly ground black pepper**
- [ ] **2 tablespoons chopped fresh parsley**

1   Melt butter in a frypan and cook bacon over a medium heat for 2 minutes. Add spring onions (shallots) and cook for 1 minute longer.

2   Add liver and sage and cook over a high heat for 2 minutes or until liver changes colour. Transfer to a warm dish and set aside to keep warm.

3   Stir wine into pan, bring to the boil and boil rapidly until almost evaporated, scraping any sediment from the base of the pan. Return livers to pan, add mushrooms and cook for 2 minutes longer. Season to taste with black pepper and mix parsley through.

VEAL CHOPS WITH SUN-DRIED TOMATOES

Sun-dried tomatoes are becoming increasingly popular and are available from most delicatessens.

Serves 4

- [ ] **8 veal chops, trimmed of all visible fat**
- [ ] **seasoned flour**
- [ ] **60 g (2 oz) butter**
- [ ] **1 clove garlic, crushed**
- [ ] **6 slices prosciutto, chopped**
- [ ] **2 tablespoons chopped fresh rosemary**
- [ ] **250 mL (8 fl oz) dry white wine**
- [ ] **16 sun-dried tomatoes, chopped**
- [ ] **4 tablespoons chopped fresh basil**

1   Coat chops with flour. Melt butter in a frypan and cook garlic, prosciutto and rosemary over a high heat for 2 minutes. Add chops and brown on both sides.

2   Stir in wine. Bring to the boil, reduce heat and simmer for 30 minutes or until veal is cooked.

3   Remove chops and prosciutto from pan and set aside to keep warm. Increase heat, stir in tomatoes and cook until sauce is reduced by half. Stir in basil and spoon sauce over chops and top with prosciutto.

CHICKEN WITH ROASTED PEPPERS

The special flavour of this dish is created by roasting peppers. Serve with pasta tossed in freshly grated Parmesan cheese.

Serves 4

- [ ] **1.5 kg (3 lb) chicken pieces**
- [ ] **freshly ground black pepper**
- [ ] **5 tablespoons olive oil**
- [ ] **1 onion, chopped**
- [ ] **2 cloves garlic, crushed**
- [ ] **2 green peppers, quartered, seeded, roasted and skins removed**
- [ ] **2 teaspoons dried rosemary**
- [ ] **6 tomatoes, peeled and quartered**
- [ ] **1 eggplant (aubergine), thinly sliced**

1   Season chicken with black pepper. Heat 2 tablespoons oil in a frypan and brown chicken on all sides. Remove from pan and set aside.

2   Add onion and garlic and cook for 3 minutes. Stir in peppers, rosemary and tomatoes and cook for 3 minutes longer.

3   Return chicken to the pan, cover and simmer for 30 minutes or until cooked. Baste chicken frequently during cooking.

4   Heat remaining oil in a frypan and cook eggplant (aubergine) slices until golden on both sides. To serve, arrange chicken and eggplant (aubergine) on a serving plate, remove green pepper from pan using a slotted spoon, and arrange on platter with chicken. Bring sauce in pan to the boil and boil for 3 minutes or until sauce is slightly thickened. Spoon over chicken and serve.

Chicken with Roasted Peppers, Veal Chops with Sun-Dried Tomatoes, Liver with Sage and Mushrooms

Fabric Made Where *Background* The Bay House Studio
Plate J.D. Milner *Silver Goblet, Plate and Tureen*
Georg Jenson

STUFFED COLD BREAST OF VEAL

Serves 8

- ☐ 2.5 kg (5 lb) breast of veal, boned and sewn up on two sides to form a pocket

STUFFING
- ☐ 3 slices white bread, crusts removed
- ☐ 125 mL (4 fl oz) milk
- ☐ 30 g (1 oz) butter
- ☐ 1 small onion, finely chopped
- ☐ 125 g (4 oz) boneless pork, minced twice
- ☐ 125 g (4 oz) boneless veal, minced twice
- ☐ 125 g (4 oz) fresh pork fat, minced twice
- ☐ 1 small calf's sweetbreads, blanched for 10 minutes then chopped
- ☐ 60 g (2 oz) grated fresh Parmesan cheese
- ☐ 250 g (8 oz) spinach leaves, cooked, well drained and chopped
- ☐ 1/4 teaspoon dried marjoram
- ☐ 1/4 teaspoon dried thyme
- ☐ 2 teaspoons salt
- ☐ 1 egg, lightly beaten
- ☐ 60 g (2 oz) shelled pistachio nuts
- ☐ 185 g (6 oz) peas
- ☐ 2 hard-boiled eggs, peeled

STOCK
- ☐ veal bones and trimmings
- ☐ 1 onion, halved
- ☐ 3 cloves garlic
- ☐ 1 carrot, roughly chopped
- ☐ 1 bay leaf
- ☐ 2 sprigs fresh parsley
- ☐ 3 litres (5 1/4 pt) chicken stock
- ☐ water
- ☐ freshly ground black pepper

1   To make stuffing, soak bread in milk for 10 minutes. Melt butter in a small frypan and cook onion over a medium heat, stirring for 5 minutes or until transparent. Remove to a large bowl and mix with pork, veal, pork fat, sweetbreads, Parmesan cheese, spinach, marjoram, thyme, salt and egg. Mix well. Knead using your hands until the mixture is fluffy and well incorporated. Remove bread from milk and squeeze dry. Mix into meat mixture. Fold in pistachios and peas.

2   Spoon half the filling into veal pocket. Top with eggs, placing them in a lengthways row. Spoon in remaining stuffing to completely cover eggs. Sew up pocket opening, using strong string.

3   To make stock, place veal bones and trimmings, onion, garlic, carrot, bay leaf and parsley in a large saucepan. Lay veal on vegetables and then pour stock over and enough water to cover veal. Season to taste with black pepper. Bring to the boil, reduce heat, cover and simmer for 1 1/4 hours, or until veal is tender.

4   Remove veal, place in a large shallow dish and set aside to cool at room temperature. Cover and refrigerate until meat is completely cold. Serve cut into 3 mm (1/8 in) slices.

BRAISED CHICKEN WITH ANCHOVY SAUCE

Serves 4

- ☐ 1.5 kg (3 lb) chicken, jointed
- ☐ freshly ground black pepper
- ☐ 1 1/2 tablespoons olive oil
- ☐ 1 small onion, finely chopped
- ☐ 1 clove garlic, finely chopped
- ☐ 125 mL (4 fl oz) dry white wine
- ☐ 1 1/2 tablespoons white wine vinegar
- ☐ 125 mL (4 fl oz) chicken stock
- ☐ 1/2 teaspoon dried oregano
- ☐ 1 bay leaf
- ☐ 1 tablespoon slivered black olives
- ☐ 3 flat anchovy fillets, rinsed in cold water, dried and chopped
- ☐ 2 tablespoons chopped parsley

1   Wash chicken under cold running water, then pat dry with absorbent kitchen paper. Season to taste with black pepper.

2   Heat oil in a heavy-based frypan and cook chicken a few pieces at a time, until brown on both sides. Remove from pan and set aside. Drain off pan juices and discard.

3   Add onion and garlic to pan and cook, stirring constantly, for 5 minutes or until lightly browned. Stir in wine and vinegar, bring to the boil and simmer until reduced to 3 tablespoons.

4   Pour in chicken stock and boil stirring constantly, for 2 minutes. Return chicken to the pan, add oregano and bay leaf. Bring to the boil, cover and simmer for 30 minutes or until tender.

5   Remove chicken pieces from pan and set aside to keep warm. Remove and discard bay leaf. Bring stock to the boil and boil until slightly thickened. Stir in olives, anchovies and parsley and cook for 1 minute longer, then spoon over chicken.

PARMESAN CHEESE

Many of the recipes in this book use fresh Parmesan cheese, available from continental delicatessens and some supermarkets. Fresh Parmesan is best purchased in a piece then grated as required. Once you have tried fresh Parmesan you will never bother with the grated powder that comes in packets. The flavour of fresh Parmesan is much milder and the texture not as grainy. If fresh Parmesan is unavailable and you must use the packaged Parmesan, about a third of the quantity is required and in a sauce you will notice its more grainy texture.

VEAL WITH SAGE AND ARTICHOKES

In this recipe fresh artichokes have been used, but if unavailable substitute with canned artichokes.

Serves 4

- ☐ 2 globe artichokes, hard tips removed
- ☐ 8 small thin slices veal
- ☐ seasoned flour
- ☐ 8 slices ham, cut to same size as veal
- ☐ 16 fresh sage leaves
- ☐ 1 tablespoon olive oil
- ☐ 185 mL (6 fl oz) dry white wine
- ☐ 60 g (2 oz) butter
- ☐ 4 tablespoons cream (single)

1   Cook artichokes in boiling water for 40 minutes or until tender. Drain, rinse under cold running water and tear leaves from bulb and discard stem.

2   Coat veal with flour. Place a ham slice and 2 sage leaves on top of each veal slice and secure with toothpicks.

3   Heat oil in frypan and cook veal over a high heat for 2 minutes each side. Remove veal from pan and set aside to keep warm.

4   Add wine to pan, bring to the boil and boil until reduced by half. Stir in artichokes, butter and cream and cook gently to heat artichokes and sauce. Spoon sauce over veal and serve.

Braised Chicken with Anchovy Sauce, Veal with Sage and Artichokes, Stuffed Cold Breast of Veal

Plates, Glasses and Fabric Made Where

VEGETABLES
and
SALADS

In Italy, vegetables are often ordered as separate side dishes, and much importance is attached to their taste and appearance. Salads are also treated with growing reverence and innovation these days. Read on for some great ideas.

❖

SPICY ASPARAGUS WITH PINE NUTS

This recipe makes a delicious entree. Use bacon instead of salami for a less spicy flavour.

Serves 4

- ☐ **500 g (1 lb) fresh asparagus spears, trimmed and cut into 5 cm (2 in) pieces**
- ☐ **15 g (¹/₂ oz) butter**
- ☐ **60 g (2 oz) pine nuts**
- ☐ **125 g (4 oz) hot Italian salami, cut into 5 mm (¹/₄ in) cubes**
- ☐ **2 tablespoons chopped fresh basil**
- ☐ **3 tablespoons grated fresh Parmesan cheese**

1 Steam or microwave asparagus until just tender. Drain and rinse under cold running water to refresh, then drain again and set aside.
2 Heat butter in a frypan and cook pine nuts and salami until lightly browned. Add asparagus and basil and cook, stirring constantly for 1 minute or until heated through. Sprinkle with Parmesan cheese and serve immediately.

❖

RADICCHIO ANCHOVY SALAD

Serves 6

- ☐ **1 radicchio lettuce, washed and leaves separated**
- ☐ **¹/₂ bunch curly endive, washed and leaves separated**
- ☐ **1 witloof (chicory), washed and leaves separated**
- ☐ **8 radishes, washed and sliced**
- ☐ **3 tablespoons chopped fresh Italian flat leaf parsley**

DRESSING
- ☐ **60 mL (2 fl oz) olive oil**
- ☐ **60 mL (2 fl oz) lemon juice**
- ☐ **60 mL (2 fl oz) dry white wine**
- ☐ **3 anchovy fillets, drained and chopped**
- ☐ **1 clove garlic, crushed**
- ☐ **¹/₂ teaspoon sugar**

1 Arrange radicchio, endive and witloof (chicory) attractively on a large platter. Top with radishes and parsley.
2 To make dressing, place oil, lemon juice, wine, anchovies, garlic and sugar in a food processor or blender and process until smooth. Just before serving, drizzle dressing over salad.

FENNEL AND ORANGE SALAD

Serves 6

- [ ] **1 bunch curly endive, leaves separated and washed**
- [ ] **1 small fennel bulb, cut into thin strips**
- [ ] **3 oranges, peeled and segmented**
- [ ] **1 onion, sliced**
- [ ] **20 black olives**

ORANGE DRESSING
- [ ] **3$^1/_2$ tablespoons olive oil**
- [ ] **3 tablespoons white wine vinegar**
- [ ] **1 tablespoon chopped fresh fennel leaves**
- [ ] **$^1/_2$ teaspoon grated orange rind**
- [ ] **$^1/_2$ teaspoon sugar**
- [ ] **freshly ground black pepper**

1   Place endive on a large serving platter. Arrange fennel, oranges, onion and olives attractively over endive.

2   To make dressing, place oil, vinegar, fennel leaves, orange rind, sugar and black pepper to taste in a screw-top jar. Shake well to combine. Pour dressing over salad and serve immediately.

FENNEL

❖   The aniseed-flavoured fennel also known as Florence fennel or finocchio, was much esteemed by the Romans, who used it to flavour many of their dishes.

❖   The feathery leaves and aromatic seeds add zing to vegetables, salad dressings, pickles and sauces, and taste delicious as a traditional accompaniment to fish.

❖   Fennel has a strong aniseed flavour but you will find when it is cooked that it loses the aniseed flavour.

Radicchio Anchovy Salad, Fennel and Orange Salad, Spicy Asparagus with Pine Nuts

Bowls Saywell Imports *Fabric and Tie Back* Boyac Decorative Furnishings *Print* Made Where *Table* Corso de Fiori

Plates J.D. Milner *Floor Ware* Collingwood Floors *Tie Back* Boyac Decorative Furnishings

SALAD SUPREMO

Serves 6

- [ ] **1 cos lettuce, washed and leaves separated and torn**
- [ ] **250 g (8 oz) cherry tomatoes**
- [ ] **1 green pepper, sliced**
- [ ] **4 hard-boiled eggs, quartered**
- [ ] **12 black olives**
- [ ] **2 teaspoons capers**
- [ ] **1 tablespoon oil**
- [ ] **125 g (4 oz) pepperoni sausage, diced**
- [ ] **2 slices white bread, cut into 1 cm (1/2 in) cubes**

DRESSING
- [ ] **3 tablespoons cider vinegar**
- [ ] **3 tablespoons vegetable oil**
- [ ] **1/4 teaspoon sugar**
- [ ] **1 clove garlic, crushed**
- [ ] **1 tablespoon chopped fresh oregano**

1   Arrange lettuce, tomatoes, green pepper, eggs, olives and capers attractively on a large platter.

2   Heat oil in a frypan and cook pepperoni and bread for 5 minutes or until bread is crisp and golden. Remove from pan and drain on absorbent kitchen paper. Set aside to cool, then sprinkle over salad.

3   To make dressing, combine vinegar, oil, sugar, garlic and oregano in a screw-top jar. Shake well to combine. Pour over salad and serve immediately.

MUSHROOM FRITTATA

Serves 6

- [ ] **15 g (1/2 oz) butter**
- [ ] **125 g (4 oz) baby mushrooms, thinly sliced**
- [ ] **2 bacon rashers, chopped**
- [ ] **1 large onion, finely chopped**
- [ ] **6 eggs**
- [ ] **5 tablespoons grated fresh Parmesan cheese**
- [ ] **2 teaspoons plain flour**
- [ ] **2 tablespoons chopped fresh Italian flat leaf parsley**

1   Melt butter in a frypan and cook mushrooms, bacon and onion for 4-5 minutes or until onion softens. Remove from pan and drain on absorbent kitchen paper.

2   Place eggs, 3 tablespoons Parmesan cheese, flour and parsley in a large bowl and beat to combine. Stir in mushroom mixture. Pour into a greased 20 cm (8 in) pie plate and bake at 180°C (350°F/Gas 4) for 10 minutes. Remove frittata from the oven and stir gently to distribute mushrooms evenly through mixture. Sprinkle remaining Parmesan cheese over and cook for 10-15 minutes or until set. Serve immediately.

Salad Supremo, Mushroom Frittata

VEGETABLE FRITTERS WITH HERB DRESSING

Serves 4

- ☐ ¹/₂ head cauliflower, cut into small florets
- ☐ 1 eggplant (aubergine)
- ☐ salt
- ☐ 1 large red pepper, seeded and cut into strips
- ☐ cornflour

BATTER
- ☐ 75 g (2¹/₂ oz) plain flour
- ☐ 3 tablespoons self-raising flour
- ☐ 250mL (8 fl oz) water
- ☐ 1 egg, lightly beaten
- ☐ oil for cooking

HERB DRESSING
- ☐ 125 mL (4 fl oz) low-oil Italian dressing
- ☐ 1 tablespoon chopped fresh basil
- ☐ 1 tablespoon chopped fresh oregano
- ☐ 1 small red chilli, seeded and finely chopped

1   Steam, boil or microwave cauliflower until just tender. Drain well and set aside. Cut eggplant (aubergine) in half lengthways and slice into 1 cm (¹/₂ in) slices. Sprinkle with salt and set aside for 30 minutes. Rinse eggplant (aubergine) under cold running water and pat dry with absorbent kitchen paper.

2   Toss cauliflower, eggplant (aubergine) and red pepper in cornflour. Shake off any excess cornflour.

3   To make batter, place plain and self-raising flours, water and egg in a food processor or blender and process until smooth. Heat oil in a large saucepan. Dip vegetables in batter and cook a few at a time in oil until golden. Remove from oil and drain on absorbent kitchen paper.

4   To make dressing, combine Italian dressing, basil, oregano and chilli in a screw-top jar and shake well. Transfer to a bowl and serve with vegetables.

❖

RICOTTA AND HERB ZUCCHINI (COURGETTES)

Serves 6

- ☐ 6 large zucchini (courgettes)

FILLING
- ☐ 30 g (1 oz) breadcrumbs made from stale bread
- ☐ 60 g (2 oz) mozzarella cheese, grated
- ☐ 125 g (4 oz) ricotta cheese
- ☐ 3 tablespoons grated fresh Parmesan cheese
- ☐ 1 tablespoon chopped fresh basil
- ☐ 2 teaspoons chopped fresh oregano
- ☐ 1 egg white, lightly beaten

1   Blanch zucchini (courgettes) until just tender. Refresh under cold running water and pat dry with absorbent kitchen paper. Cut almost through each zucchini (courgette) crossways at 2 cm (³/₄ in) intervals, taking care not to cut right through.

2   To make filling, combine breadcrumbs, mozzarella cheese, ricotta cheese, Parmesan cheese, basil and oregano in a bowl. Stir in egg white and mix well. Place some filling in each zucchini (courgette) cut. Place zucchini (courgettes) in baking dish, brush lightly with oil and cook at 240°C (475°F/Gas 8) for 15 minutes, or until heated through and filling browns.

Ricotta and Herb Zucchini (Courgettes), Vegetable Fritters with Herb Dressing

MILANESE-STYLE FENNEL

This dish can be made a day ahead of serving then reheated when required.

Serves 6

- ☐ **2 large fennel bulbs, trimmed and cut into 1 cm (1/2 in) strips**

SAUCE
- ☐ **30 g (1 oz) butter**
- ☐ **2 tablespoons plain flour**
- ☐ **375 mL (12 fl oz) skim milk**
- ☐ **1/4 teaspoon ground (grated) nutmeg**
- ☐ **freshly ground black pepper**

TOPPING
- ☐ **60 g (2 oz) breadcrumbs, made from stale bread**
- ☐ **3 tablespoons grated fresh Parmesan cheese**
- ☐ **30 g (1 oz) butter, melted**
- ☐ **paprika**

1 Boil, steam or microwave fennel until tender. Drain and set aside.

2 To make sauce, melt butter in a saucepan, add flour and cook for 1 minute. Remove from heat and gradually stir in milk. Cook over a medium heat, stirring constantly, until sauce boils and thickens. Add nutmeg and season to taste with black pepper.

3 To make topping, combine breadcrumbs, Parmesan cheese and butter. Arrange fennel in a shallow ovenproof dish, pour sauce over and sprinkle with topping. Dust with paprika and bake at 200°C (400°F/Gas 6) for 15-20 minutes or until browned.

MICROWAVE IT

To make the sauce in the microwave, melt butter in a microwave-safe jug, stir in flour then gradually stir in milk. Cook on HIGH (100%) for 3 minutes, or until sauce boils and thickens. Stir twice during cooking.

ARTICHOKE SALAD WITH PESTO DRESSING

Serves 6

- ☐ **1 bunch watercress, washed**
- ☐ **410 g (13 oz) canned artichoke hearts, drained**
- ☐ **4 tomatoes, peeled and diced**
- ☐ **2 bocconcini cheese, sliced**

PESTO DRESSING
- ☐ **60 g (2 oz) fresh basil leaves**
- ☐ **3 tablespoons olive oil**
- ☐ **1 clove garlic, crushed**
- ☐ **3 tablespoons grated fresh Parmesan cheese**
- ☐ **2 tablespoons pine nuts, toasted**

1 Break watercress into small pieces and place in a bowl. Arrange artichokes, tomatoes and bocconcini cheese over watercress.

2 To make dressing, place basil, oil, garlic, Parmesan cheese and pine nuts in a food processor or blender and process until smooth. Drizzle over salad and toss gently to coat salad ingredients.

SPINACH AND RAISINS ALLA LIGURIA

Serves 4

- ☐ **1 bunch (500 g/1 lb) spinach, stalks removed**
- ☐ **30 g (1 oz) butter**
- ☐ **1 clove garlic, crushed**
- ☐ **4 slices prosciutto, chopped**
- ☐ **3 tablespoons raisins, chopped**
- ☐ **1 tablespoon chopped fresh thyme**
- ☐ **freshly ground black pepper**
- ☐ **3 tablespoons pine nuts, toasted**

1 Boil, steam or microwave spinach until just tender. Drain well and chop roughly.

2 Heat butter in a frypan. Cook garlic and prosciutto, stirring, for 1 minute. Add spinach, raisins and thyme and cook, stirring, for 2-3 minutes longer or until heated through. Season to taste with black pepper and transfer to a serving dish. Sprinkle with pine nuts and serve immediately.

COOK'S TIP

You can substitute dried cannellini beans if you wish. Cook following directions on the packet to give about 585 g (1 1/4 lb) of cooked beans.

ITALIAN BEAN HOTPOT

This recipe is quick and easy to prepare. Served with fresh crusty bread and a salad it makes a perfect luncheon or supper dish.

Serves 6

- ☐ **2 tablespoons olive oil**
- ☐ **2 cloves garlic, crushed**
- ☐ **1 onion, sliced**
- ☐ **1 tablespoon chopped fresh sage, or 1 teaspoon dried sage leaves**
- ☐ **2 x 315 g (10 oz) canned cannellini beans, drained**
- ☐ **410 g (13 oz) canned peppers, drained and thinly sliced**
- ☐ **440 g (14 oz) canned tomatoes, undrained and chopped**
- ☐ **440 g (14 oz) canned tomato puree (passata)**
- ☐ **2 zucchini (courgettes), sliced**
- ☐ **freshly ground black pepper**
- ☐ **3 tablespoons grated fresh Parmesan cheese**

1 Heat oil in a frypan and cook garlic, onion and sage for 4-5 minutes or until onion softens.

2 Stir in beans, peppers, tomatoes, tomato puree (passata) and zucchini (courgettes). Bring to the boil, reduce heat and simmer uncovered for 15 minutes or until mixture reduces and thickens. Season to taste with black pepper and sprinkle with Parmesan cheese.

Milanese-Style Fennel, Artichoke Salad with Pesto Dressing, Spinach and Raisins Alla Liguria, Italian Bean Hotpot

Fabric Made Where Wooden Bowl Fruit Stand and Salt and Pepper Bibelot Column and Glass Corso de Fiori Painting The Bay House Studio

DESSERTS
and
CAKES

How 'dolce' it is, that final course. When you see what treats are in store for dessert, you might just decide to serve nothing but these creamy, sugary, crunchy, divinely indulgent delights.

❖

COUNTRY PEAR CAKE

Serves 6

- ☐ **2 eggs**
- ☐ **200 g (6¹/₂ oz) sugar**
- ☐ **4 tablespoons milk**
- ☐ **200 g (6¹/₂ oz) self-raising flour, sifted**
- ☐ **25 g (¹/₂ oz) dried breadcrumbs**
- ☐ **2 pears, peeled, cored and sliced**
- ☐ **30 g (1 oz) butter**
- ☐ **60 g (2 oz) flaked almonds**

1   Beat eggs and sugar in a mixing bowl until light and fluffy. Fold through milk alternately with flour.
2   Sprinkle a greased and lined 23 cm (9 in) round cake pan (tin) with breadcrumbs. Spoon half the batter into pan (tin) and arrange pear slices on top. Pour remaining batter over. Dot with butter and sprinkle with almonds. Bake at 180°C (350°F/Gas 4) for 30-35 minutes or until cooked when tested with a skewer.

❖

TOFFEE ORANGES

Serves 6

- ☐ **6 oranges**
- ☐ **90 g (3 oz) sugar**
- ☐ **60 mL (2 fl oz) Grand Marnier**
- ☐ **4 whole cloves**
- ☐ **1 cinnamon stick**

TOFFEE
- ☐ **500 g (1 lb) sugar**
- ☐ **170 mL (5¹/₂ fl oz) water**

1   Cut 10 long thin strips of peel from oranges, using a sharp knife or vegetable peeler. Cut peel into smaller strips and blanch in boiling water. Drain and reserve liquid.
2   Remove remaining peel and pith from oranges and discard. Place oranges in a bowl with sugar, Grand Marnier, 60 mL (2 fl oz) reserved blanching liquid, cloves and cinnamon stick. Cover and refrigerate overnight.
3   To make toffee, place sugar and water in a saucepan. Cook over a medium heat, stirring constantly until sugar dissolves. Bring to the boil. Continue to cook, without stirring, until a light golden colour. Arrange oranges on a serving platter, drizzle toffee over and top with strips of peel.

❖

FIG ICE CREAM

Serves 6

- ☐ **500 g (1 lb) dried figs, trimmed**
- ☐ **125 g (4 oz) sugar**
- ☐ **250 mL (8 fl oz) water**
- ☐ **125 mL (4 fl oz) milk**
- ☐ **125 mL (4 fl oz) cream (single)**

1   Place figs and sugar in a food processor or blender and process until smooth and creamy. Add water, milk and cream and continue to process until combined.
2   Transfer mixture to an ice cream maker and freeze according to the manufacturer's instructions.

Fig Ice Cream, Toffee Oranges, Country Pear Cake

Basket G & C Ventura *Cup and Saucer* Lifestyle Imports *Glass* Ah Ah Do Do *Glass bowl and Wooden tray* Interim *Fabric* Boyac Decorative Furnishings

FROZEN ZABAGLIONE

This version of zabaglione is flavoured with rum, cognac, coffee and chocolate.

Serves 6

- ☐ **5 egg yolks**
- ☐ **125 g (4 oz) caster sugar**
- ☐ **2 tablespoons rum**
- ☐ **2 tablespoons cognac**
- ☐ **4 tablespoons dry Marsala**
- ☐ **250 mL (8 fl oz) thickened cream (double), lightly whipped**
- ☐ **4 egg whites**
- ☐ **125 g (4 oz) icing sugar**
- ☐ **2 teaspoons instant coffee, dissolved in 1 tablespoon water**
- ☐ **60 g (2 oz) dark chocolate, grated**

1   Place egg yolks and sugar in the top of a double saucepan and whisk until pale and thick and the mixture forms a ribbon.
2   Combine rum, cognac and Marsala and gradually whisk into egg yolk mixture. Place top of double saucepan over simmering water and whisk until mixture becomes soft and foamy. Remove from heat and set aside to cool. Fold cream through egg mixture.
3   Beat egg whites until soft peaks form, gradually add icing sugar and continue beating until combined. Fold 2 tablespoons egg white mixture through egg yolk mixture, then gently fold through remaining egg white mixture. Place one-third mixture in a bowl and mix in coffee mixture. Fold chocolate through remaining mixture.
4   Spoon half chocolate mixture into a 10 x 25 cm (4 x 10 in) loaf pan (tin) lined with tin foil, smooth top with a spatula and freeze until firm. Spoon coffee mixture over, level with a spatula and return to freezer until this layer firms. Spread remaining chocolate mixture over, level with a spatula and return to freezer. Freeze overnight.

❖

ESPRESSO GRANITA

Serves 4

- ☐ **500 mL (16 fl oz) strong black coffee**
- ☐ **90 g (3 oz) sugar**
- ☐ **250 mL (8 fl oz) thickened cream (double), whipped with 1 tablespoon sugar**

1   Combine coffee and sugar, stirring until sugar dissolves completely. Pour into a 28 x 18 cm (11 x 7 in) shallow cake pan (tin). Freeze until just beginning to set,

Plates Ah Ah Do Do Bowl Italia Line 2002

then stir with a fork, scraping in the edges. Return to the freezer and freeze until firm.

2   Transfer granita to a food processor or blender and process quickly. Return mixture to pan (tin) and freeze for 1 hour. Remove from freezer 10 minutes prior to serving and place in the refrigerator. Stir to make a fine icy granulation and spoon into glasses. To serve, top with cream.

❖

STRAWBERRIES IN BALSAMIC VINEGAR

The vinegar enhances the natural sweetness of the strawberries and leaves a wonderful aftertaste.

Serves 4

☐ **1 kg (2 lb) strawberries, washed and hulled**
☐ **4 tablespoons sugar**
☐ **2 tablespoons balsamic vinegar**

Place strawberries and sugar in a bowl. Toss to combine, cover and refrigerate for 1 hour. Stir vinegar through and serve in chilled glasses.

❖

GRILLED FRUITS WITH COGNAC MASCARPONE

Any fresh fruits can be served this way.

Serves 4

☐ **250 g (8 oz) blueberries**
☐ **250 g (8 oz) strawberries, hulled and halved**
☐ **4 peaches, peeled and quartered**
☐ **250 g (8 oz) raspberries**
☐ **125 g (4 oz) brown sugar**
☐ **750 g (1½ lb) mascarpone**
☐ **2 tablespoons caster sugar**
☐ **60 mL (2 fl oz) cognac**

1   Combine blueberries, strawberries, peaches and raspberries in a bowl. Place fruit in a shallow ovenproof dish and sprinkle with brown sugar. Cook under a hot grill for 8 minutes or until sugar melts and caramelises.

2   To serve, place a mound of mascarpone on each serving plate, make a well in the centre, sprinkle with caster sugar and fill well with cognac. Surround with hot fruit and serve immediately.

Left: Strawberries in Balsamic Vinegar, Frozen Zabaglione
Right: Espresso Granita, Grilled Fruits with Cognac Mascarpone

Vase Corso de Fiori Tassel Sandy de Beyer Fabric Boyac Decorative Furnishings

POACHED PEARS WITH CHAMPAGNE ZABAGLIONE

This version of zabaglione is a little thinner than the traditional version due to the amount of champagne added.

Serves 4

- ☐ **4 pears, stalks attached and peeled**
- ☐ **60 mL (2 fl oz) lemon juice**
- ☐ **185 g (6 oz) sugar**
- ☐ **600 mL (1 pt) champagne or dry sparkling wine**

ZABAGLIONE
- ☐ **4 egg yolks**
- ☐ **3 tablespoons caster sugar**
- ☐ **375 mL (12 fl oz) champagne or dry sparkling wine**

1 Brush pears with lemon juice and place in a saucepan with the sugar and champagne. Bring to the boil, cover and simmer for 20-30 minutes or until pears are soft. Baste pears several times during cooking. Remove pan from heat and set aside to cool.

2 To make zabaglione, whisk egg yolks and sugar in the top of a double saucepan until thick and pale. Place top of double saucepan over simmering water and gradually whisk in champagne. Continue whisking over a gentle heat until zabaglione thickens.

3 Remove pears from poaching liquid and set aside. Cook poaching liquid over a high heat until thick and syrupy. To serve, divide zabaglione between serving plates, top with pears and drizzle syrup over.

❖

AMARETTI

Amaretti are the almond macaroons used as a base for many Italian desserts, or simply served with gelato, ice cream or a cup of strong espresso coffee.

Makes 80

- ☐ **3 egg whites**
- ☐ **250 g (8 oz) caster sugar**
- ☐ **250 g (8 oz) ground almonds**
- ☐ **4 tablespoons icing sugar**

1 Beat egg whites until soft peaks form. Add sugar a little at a time, beating well after each addition, until mixture is thick and glossy. Fold almonds and 2 tablespoons icing sugar through mixture.

2 Place mixture in a piping bag fitted with a large plain nozzle and pipe small oval lengths onto an oven tray lined with baking paper. Dust with remaining icing sugar and bake at 160°C (325°F/Gas 3) for 15 minutes or until lightly browned. Allow to cool on tray, before removing paper and storing in an airtight container.

Poached Pears with Champagne Zabaglione, Amaretti

Bowl Saywell *Moon Dish* Interim

Tea Set G & C Ventura

APRICOT ALMOND SHORTCAKE

Serves 8

- ☐ **125 g (4 oz) butter**
- ☐ **125 g (4 oz) sugar**
- ☐ **1 egg**
- ☐ **90 g (3 oz) self-raising flour, sifted**
- ☐ **90 g (3 oz) plain flour, sifted**

ALMOND APRICOT FILLING

- ☐ **45 g (1¹/₂ oz) butter**
- ☐ **2 tablespoons caster sugar**
- ☐ **1 egg yolk**
- ☐ **90 g (3 oz) ground almonds**
- ☐ **2 teaspoons plain flour**
- ☐ **440 g (14 oz) canned apricots, drained**

TOPPING

- ☐ **410 g (13 oz) ground almonds**
- ☐ **5 tablespoons caster sugar**
- ☐ **6 eggs, separated**
- ☐ **2 tablespoons Amaretto liqueur**
- ☐ **250 g (8 oz) apricot jam, warmed and sieved**
- ☐ **60 g (2oz) flaked almonds, toasted**

1   Place butter and sugar in a large mixing bowl and beat until light and creamy. Add egg and beat well, stir in self-raising and plain flours. Turn out onto a lightly floured surface and knead lightly until smooth. Divide mixture into two equal portions and refrigerate for 30 minutes.

2   Roll out each portion between sheets of plastic food wrap or greaseproof paper to a 20 cm (8 in) circle. Press one circle dough into a greased and lined 20 cm (8 in) deep cake pan (tin).

3   To make filling, place butter, sugar and egg yolk in a small bowl and beat until light and fluffy. Stir in almonds and flour. Place apricots in a food processor or blender and process until smooth. Swirl apricots through almond mixture. Take care not to over mix. Spread mixture over dough in cake pan, leaving a small border around edge. Place second circle of dough over apricot mixture and press edges together. Brush with water and bake at 180°C (350°F/Gas 4) for 35-40 minutes. Stand 15 minutes before turning out on a wire rack to cool.

4   To make topping, place almonds and sugar in a mixing bowl. Combine egg yolks and Amaretto in a small bowl, then gradually stir into almond mixture. Remove one-third of mixture and set aside. Add 1 tablespoon of unbeaten egg white to remaining mixture and spread over sides and top of shortcake. Add a little more egg white if mixture is difficult to spread.

5   Add 2 tablespoons of unbeaten egg white to reserved almond mixture and spoon into a piping bag fitted with a large star nozzle. Pipe lines in a zigzag pattern over top and pipe small rosettes around the edge. Place cake on an oven tray and bake at 250°C (500°F/Gas 9) for 8-10 minutes or until top is lightly browned. Spoon two-thirds of jam between zigzag piping and set aside for 10 minutes to cool slightly. Spread sides with remaining jam and coat with toasted almonds. Cool cake completely before cutting.

Apricot Almond Shortcake

CHERRY TART

This tart is equally as good made using any preserved fruit. You might like to try using peaches, apricots or pears.

Serves 8

- ☐ **250 g (8 oz) plain flour, sifted**
- ☐ **125 g (4 oz) sugar**
- ☐ **125 g (4 oz) butter, melted and cooled**
- ☐ **2 tablespoons milk**
- ☐ **1 teaspoon grated lemon rind**
- ☐ **2 egg yolks, lightly beaten**
- ☐ **2 x 440 g (14 oz) canned cherries, drained**
- ☐ **125 g (4 oz) peach or apricot conserve, warmed and sieved**

1 Combine flour and sugar in a bowl and make a well in the centre. Add butter, milk, lemon rind and egg yolks and mix, using a knife. Knead lightly until dough is smooth, wrap in plastic food wrap and refrigerate for 30 minutes. Roll out two-thirds of dough into a rectangle 1 cm (¹/₂ in) thick, between two sheets of plastic food wrap. Line a greased 10 x 35 cm (4 x 14 in) tin with pastry. Arrange cherries in rows on pastry.
2 Place remaining dough into a piping bag fitted with a plain nozzle and pipe long strips of dough over cherries in a lattice pattern. Pinch edges of pastry strips and base together.
3 Bake at 180°C (350°F/Gas 4) for 25-30 minutes or until golden. Brush warm tart with conserve and serve warm or chilled.

❖

ALMOND RICOTTA CHEESECAKE

A light baked cheesecake that can be served warm or chilled. This cake looks great decorated with chocolate leaves.

Serves 8

PASTRY
- ☐ **250 g (8 oz) plain flour, sifted**
- ☐ **125 g (4 oz) butter**
- ☐ **1 egg yolk**
- ☐ **1 tablespoon cold water**

FILLING
- ☐ **750 g (1¹/₂ lb) ricotta cheese**
- ☐ **125 g (4 oz) sugar**
- ☐ **90 g (3 oz) ground almonds**
- ☐ **1 teaspoon grated lemon rind**
- ☐ **¹/₂ teaspoon vanilla essence**
- ☐ **4 eggs**

TOPPING
- ☐ **250 mL (8 fl oz) cream (single)**
- ☐ **1 tablespoon Amaretto liqueur**

1 To make pastry, place flour in a bowl and rub in butter using the fingertips, until mixture resembles fine breadcrumbs. Using a knife, mix in egg yolk and water to form a firm dough. Wrap pastry in plastic food wrap and chill for 1 hour.
2 Roll out pastry and line a 23 cm (9 in) pie plate. Trim edges.
3 To make filling, combine ricotta, sugar, almonds and lemon rind in a bowl. Beat in vanilla and eggs one at a time. Spoon filling into pastry shell and bake at 200°C (400°F/Gas 6) for 5 minutes. Reduce heat to 180°C (350°F/Gas 4) and bake for 30 minutes longer, or until filling is firm.
4 To make topping, whip cream and Amaretto together until soft peaks form. Just prior to serving turn out cake and spread with topping.

❖

VENETIAN PUMPKIN FRITTERS

A light and airy fritter is a popular dessert. Traditionally served with a glass of chilled white wine, around carnival time in February.

Makes 30

- ☐ **90 g (3 oz) sultanas**
- ☐ **500 g (1 lb) pumpkin, cooked and mashed**
- ☐ **4 tablespoons sugar**
- ☐ **125 g (4 oz) self-raising flour, sifted**
- ☐ **¹/₂ teaspoon ground allspice**
- ☐ **1 teaspoon grated orange rind**
- ☐ **2 eggs, separated**
- ☐ **oil for cooking**
- ☐ **1 teaspoon ground cinnamon**

1 Cover sultanas with cold water and set aside to soak for 15 minutes. Drain and pat dry. Place pumpkin, 2 tablespoons sugar, flour, orange rind, sultanas, egg yolks and allspice in a bowl and mix to combine. Beat egg whites until soft peaks form. Fold through pumpkin mixture.
2 Heat oil in a saucepan to 195°C (385°F) and cook teaspoons of mixture until crisp and golden. Drain fritters on absorbent kitchen paper and toss in remaining sugar mixed with cinnamon. Serve warm.

Almond Ricotta Cheesecake, Cherry Tart Venetian Pumpkin Fritters

ITALIAN LIQUEURS

A liqueur is sweetened alcohol infused with fruits, herbs or nuts. The best known Italian liqueurs are Galliano, Sambuca, Amaretto and Frangelico. They are delicious after-dinner liqueurs or can be used to add flavour to desserts and sweets.

✧ Galliano is a herb flavoured liqueur, if added to mousses or gelatin desserts it not only adds a great flavour but also will give a subtle colour.

✧ Sambuca is anise flavoured liqueur and traditionally is drunk neat with three coffee beans floating on the top. Never float an even number of beans on Sambuca as this is believed to be bad luck.

✧ Amaretto is made of apricots and almonds and has a distinctive flavour. It is well known as a cocktail ingredient but is also wonderful in ice creams, trifles, custards and poured over fresh fruit.

✧ Frangelico is a delicious liqueur made from hazelnuts, berries, almonds, orange flowers and cinnamon, that comes in a uniquely shaped bottle. It was originally made by monks and much mystery and legend surrounds its origin.

❖

CASSATA SICILIANA

A simple do-ahead dinner party dessert that looks spectacular when decorated with extra glace fruit. It is best prepared a day before serving.

Serves 8

- [ ] **500 g (1 lb) ricotta cheese**
- [ ] **250 g (8 oz) sugar**
- [ ] **2 tablespoons chopped pistachios**
- [ ] **3 tablespoons chopped glace fruit**
- [ ] **$1/4$ teaspoon ground cinnamon**
- [ ] **60 g (2 oz) dark chocolate, grated**
- [ ] **2 tablespoons Amaretto liqueur**
- [ ] **20 cm (8 in) round sponge cake, cut into 1 cm ($1/2$ in) slices**

TOPPING

- [ ] **250 mL (8 fl oz) cream (single)**
- [ ] **1 tablespoon Amaretto liqueur**
- [ ] **selection glace fruit**

1   Beat ricotta and sugar together until light and fluffy. Divide mixture in half. Fold pistachios and fruit through half of mixture. Mix cinnamon, chocolate and Amaretto into other half. Cover and set aside.

2   Line base and sides of a 20 cm (8 in) bowl or mould with plastic food wrap, then with three-quarters of cake slices. Fill with ricotta mixture and cover with remaining cake. Cover and freeze for 2 hours or overnight.

3   When mixture is set pour chocolate mixture over, return to freezer and freeze until set.

4   To make topping, whip cream and Amaretto together until soft peaks form. Just prior to serving, turn out cassata, spread completely with cream and decorate with glace fruit.

❖

COFFEE SPONGE PUFFS

Serves 6

- [ ] **2 eggs**
- [ ] **125 g (4 oz) caster sugar**
- [ ] **4 tablespoons self-raising flour, sifted**
- [ ] **4 tablespoons cornflour**
- [ ] **icing sugar**

COFFEE CUSTARD FILLING

- [ ] **250 mL (8 fl oz) milk**
- [ ] **1 tablespoon instant coffee**
- [ ] **3 egg yolks**
- [ ] **60 g (2 oz) caster sugar**
- [ ] **$1^{1}/_{2}$ tablespoons flour**
- [ ] **125 mL (4 fl oz) thickened cream (double), whipped**

1   Place eggs in a mixing bowl and beat until thick and creamy. Add sugar a little at a time, beating well after each addition until mixture thickens and sugar dissolves. This will take about 10 minutes.

2   Sift flour and cornflour together then fold through egg mixture in two batches. Spoon heaped tablespoons of mixture onto lightly greased baking trays, leaving about 5 cm (2 in) between each puff. Bake at 180°C (350°F/Gas 4) for 8-10 minutes or until puffs are golden. Transfer puffs to a wire rack to cool.

3   To make filling, place milk and coffee in a saucepan and heat until almost boiling. Whisk together egg yolks, sugar and flour until thick and creamy. Gradually whisk milk mixture into egg mixture. Return mixture to saucepan and heat, stirring, until mixture thickens. Remove from heat and set aside to cool. Fold through whipped cream.

4   Spread filling over flat side of half the puffs and top with remaining puffs. Dust tops with icing sugar and serve immediately.

❖

SICILIAN ROLL

Serves 8

- [ ] **3 eggs**
- [ ] **125 g (4 oz) caster sugar**
- [ ] **90 g (3 oz) self-raising flour, sifted**
- [ ] **2 tablespoons hot milk**
- [ ] **125 g (4 fl oz) cream (single), whipped**
- [ ] **60 g (2 oz) chocolate, grated**

FILLING

- [ ] **250 g (8 oz) ricotta cheese**
- [ ] **4 tablespoons icing sugar**
- [ ] **$1/2$ teaspoon vanilla essence**
- [ ] **1 tablespoon Creme de Cacao**
- [ ] **30 g (1 oz) chocolate, grated**
- [ ] **1 tablespoon chopped glace fruit**

1   Place eggs in a large mixing bowl and beat until thick and creamy. Add sugar a little at a time, beating well after each addition until sugar dissolves and mixture thickens. Fold in flour alternately with milk.

2   Spoon mixture into a lightly greased and lined 25 x 30 cm (10 x 12 in) shallow cake pan (tin). Bake at 180°C (350°F/Gas 4) for 12-15 minutes or until firm. Turn out onto a sheet of baking paper, remove lining paper and trim edges. Roll up from the narrow end, using paper to lift and guide roll. Stand for 5 minutes, then unroll and allow to cool.

3   To make filling, place ricotta cheese, icing sugar, vanilla and Creme de Cacao in a mixing bowl and beat until well combined. Fold through chocolate and glace fruit and spread over cake. Reroll and transfer to a serving platter. Spread with cream and decorate with grated chocolate.

Cassata Siciliana, Sicilian Roll, Coffee Sponge Puffs

Table Corso de Fiori Cup and Large Platter Made in Japan *Cherub* Sandy de Beyer *Fabric* Boyac Decorative Furnishings *Ribbon* Offray

ITALIAN CHEESES

Gorgonzola, mascarpone, Parmesan, pecorino – the list of Italy's splendid cheeses is virtually endless. Different regions have developed unique cheese styles over the centuries, and whether you're cooking with an Italian cheese, adding one to a cooked dish, or assembling a cheese platter, you're dealing with some of the world's best.

The cheeses of Italy originated in the dairies and kitchens of farmers. Each region has at least one cheese peculiar to it, and this is reflected in the cooking of the region. It would be difficult to create authentic Italian dishes without having the appropriate cheese available and we are lucky that in our shops most cheese counters offer a range of both imported and locally made cheeses to choose from. Price is not always an indication of which is best, so it is a good idea to taste-test before buying.

✧ **Bel Paese**, meaning 'beautiful country', is a commercial variation of a mild, semi-soft, creamy cheese made from cows' milk and comes from the Lombardy region. It melts easily and is perfect for cooking; it can be used in place of mozzarella and fontina.

✧ **Caciocavallo** from southern Italy and Sicily is made from cows' milk sometimes mixed with goats' milk. The name means 'cheese on horseback', which refers to the way the cheeses are strung together in pairs and hung to mature over poles, as if astride a horse. When fresh, it is soft and sweet and eaten as a table cheese. When aged, it becomes spicy and tangy and should be used for grating. If unavailable, use provolone which is the more widely known member of the same family of cheeses.

✧ **Dolcelatte** is one of the Gorgonzola cheeses, see below.

✧ **Fontina** is a semi-hard cows' milk cheese with a sweet and nutty flavour. Although classified as a table cheese, it is most commonly used in fonduta, a traditional dish from the region of Piemont. If fontina is unavailable, use gruyere for a fondue, or Bel Paese or matured mozzarella for other dishes.

✧ **Gorgonzola** is produced today by introducing a harmless penicillin bacteria which causes the characteristic blue mould. Made from cows' milk, it has a soft, creamy texture and a buttery flavour. There are several kinds of Gorgonzola. Dolcelatte is the most well known, meaning 'sweet milk', it is the creamiest and sweetest variety. Dolce verde is more piquant and is stronger in flavour and smell. You can use any other creamy, mild blue-vein, or blend some cream with a sharper, crumbly blue-vein in place of Gorgonzola.

✧ **Grana** is a collective name used to describe matured, hard cheeses from northern and central Italy. These cheeses have a close grain ideal for grating. Parmesan and grana padano are the most well-known in this group of cheeses. Grana padano is made from cows' milk from areas outside those designated for reggiano production. Because of a shorter maturing time it is less flavoursome and moister than Parmesan. Wherever possible, grana cheeses should be bought in a piece to be freshly grated as required.

✧ **Mascarpone** is a fresh cheese made from cream. It is unsalted, buttery and rich with a fat content of 90 per cent and it is used mostly as a dessert, either alone or as an ingredient. If it is unavailable, mix one part thick sour cream to three parts thickened cream

(double), or beat 250 g (8 oz) ricotta cheese with 250 mL (8 fl oz) cream (single) until smooth and thick.

❖

HOMEMADE MASCARPONE CHEESE

If mascarpone cheese is unavailable this recipe makes a good alternative. You will find that the curd will form more quickly in warmer weather.

Makes 250 g (8 oz)

- ☐ **375 mL (12 fl oz) thickened cream (double)**
- ☐ **3 tablespoons buttermilk**

1   Place cream in a saucepan and heat to lukewarm (32°C/90°F). Pour into a bowl and stir in buttermilk. Cover and set aside to stand for 24-48 hours, or until a soft curd forms.
2   Dip a piece of muslin, large enough to line a colander, in cold water, then wring dry. Line colander with muslin and place in the sink. Pour curd into colander and set aside to drain for about 10 minutes.
3   Fold muslin over curd and place colander on a rack in a baking dish. Cover colander and baking dish with plastic food wrap to make airtight. Refrigerate for 36-48 hours.

✧ **Mozzarella** was once made exclusively from buffalo milk, but today cows' milk is more commonly used. Real mozzarella, when fresh and moist, is enjoyed as a table cheese. As it ages and dries, it is only good for cooking, but its excellent melting qualities are retained. Mozzarella is the traditional pizza cheese and is available in a variety of shapes and sizes, including small balls called bocconcini, and a smoked variety.
✧ **Parmesan**, or Parmigiano Reggiano, is the most famous of the grana cheeses. It is made only from cows' milk from strictly controlled areas and must be matured for at least two years. The words Parmigiano-Reggiano are imprinted all over the thick rind as proof of its authenticity. When young, the cheese is sweet and moist, as it ages the flavour becomes stronger and the texture drier. It is used for grating at any age. When served as a table cheese it is usually eaten young.
✧ **Pecorino**, made from sheep's milk (pecora means sheep) and matured for six to eight months, is saltier, sharper and more tangy than Parmesan and is used where a more piquant flavour is needed. The most common varieties are pecorino romano and pecorino sardo. Outside Italy, pecorino romano is often made from cows' milk.
✧ **Provolone** is a cooked cheese, now made from cows' milk and famous for the multitude of shapes and sizes into which it is formed. Provolone dolce is young and sweet, while provolone piccante is mature and strong. Both are used as a table cheese as well as for cooking. When unavailable, a matured gouda can be used in its place.

✧ **Ricotta** is made throughout Italy from cows', sheeps' or goats' milk, but elsewhere it is usually cows' milk which is used. It is a cooked cheese made from whey and has a very low fat content and mild flavour. Where fresh ricotta is hard to get, drained and sieved cottage cheese may be used in some dishes; or see our recipe for Homemade Ricotta Cheese.
✧ **Stracchino** is a generic name for a group of rindless fresh cheeses which have a smooth, creamy texture and mild flavour. It should be eaten as fresh as possible as it tends to sour quickly. Taleggio is probably the best known stracchino.

❖

HOMEMADE RICOTTA CHEESE

If ricotta cheese is unavailable try making this version in your own kitchen.

Makes 250 g (8 oz)

- ☐ **1 litre (1¾ pt) fresh milk**
- ☐ **1 teaspoon salt**
- ☐ **4 teaspoons lemon juice**

1   Place milk, salt and lemon juice in a saucepan. Bring to the boil then simmer for 15 minutes, or until the curds float on the top.
2   Transfer curds into a square of muslin, tie up and hang up over the sink to drain for 2-3 hours.

PERFECT ITALIAN MEALS

A clear broth, a simple pasta and a dessert of fresh figs constitutes a perfect Italian meal. So does a table groaning with antipasto, three pasta selections, a meat course, a dessert and gelati choice, a platter of cheeses and hard pears, all topped off with crunchy almond biscotti dipped in glasses of vin santo! Try some of these options.

A formal Italian meal has no real main course, rather it is a succession of courses which starts with antipasto (appetiser), is followed by the first course (primo) of pasta, risotto or soup. The second course (secondo) is meat, poultry or fish, accompanied by one or two vegetable side dishes (contorni). Salad (insalata) and sometimes cheese is then served and finally the meal ends with dessert or fruit (dolce).

It is only recently that antipasto has become so important in Italian eating. Traditionally it consisted of only a few slices of salami or cured meats and with many Italians these still remain the favourites. Remember antipasto is only a starter so do not serve too much if it is to be part of a complete meal. An antipasto platter can make a wonderful light meal in itself (see page 4).

Most Italians consider the first course to be the most important and pasta is always popular.

While the Italians have a wonderful range of desserts they seldom serve them at home, instead they would end a meal with fruit in season.

❖

PIZZA PARTY FOR EIGHT

Artichoke, Mozzarella and Salami Pizza
(page 52)

Chicken and Asparagus Calzone
(page 48)

Fried Flatbread
(page 50)

Radicchio Anchovy Salad
(page 66)

Fig Ice Cream
(page 72)

❖

PASTA DINNER FOR FOUR

Chilled Brandy Fig and Apple Soup
(page 8)

Bonbons Filled with Chicken
and Herbs
(page 24)

Salad Supremo
(page 68)

Crusty Italian Bread

Espresso Granita
(page 74)

❖

COOK AHEAD DINNER
FOR SIX

Hearty Bean and Tomato Soup
(page 9)

Rabbit-Filled Peppers
(page 59)

Mixed Lettuce and Fresh Herb Salad

Crusty Italian Bread

Cherry Tart
(page 78)

COUNTDOWN FOR COOK AHEAD DINNER

THE DAY BEFORE
✧ Make Hearty Bean and Tomato Soup.
✧ Make the filling for Rabbit-Filled Peppers and fill the peppers.
✧ Make Cherry Tart.

30 MINUTES BEFORE SERVING
✧ Make Mixed Lettuce and Fresh Herb Salad, but do not dress.
✧ Reheat soup.
✧ Complete cooking of Rabbit-Filled Peppers.

JUST PRIOR TO SERVING
✧ Dress salad.

ITALIAN SEAFOOD BARBECUE FOR SIX

Sardine Fritters
(Make 1½ recipe quantity)
(page 10)

Octopus in Red Wine Marinade
(page 10)

Lemony Prawn Kebabs
(Make 1½ recipe quantity)
(page 13)

Radicchio Anchovy Salad
(page 66)

Fennel and Orange Salad
(page 67)

Grilled Fruits with Cognac Mascarpone
(Make 1½ recipe quantity)
(page 75)

TIPS FOR ITALIAN BARBECUE

✧ The Sardine Fritters can be cooked on a hotplate or in a frypan on the barbecue.
✧ The Octopus in Red Wine Marinade can be cooked in a saucepan on the barbecue, this can be put on shortly after the barbecue has been lit and be cooking while the barbecue is heating.
✧ The grilled fruits for the Grilled Fruits with Cognac Mascarpone can be cooked on the barbecue and makes a delicious and easy dessert.

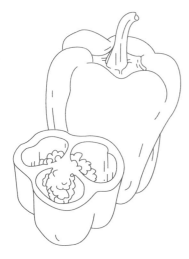

DESSERT AND COFFEE PARTY FOR SIX

Cassata Siciliana
(page 81)

Amaretti
(page 76)

Country Pear Cake
(page 72)

Coffee

QUICK AS A FLASH MEAL FOR FOUR

Fettuccine with Veal Cream Sauce
(page 31)

Mixed Lettuce and Fresh Herb Salad

Crostini
(page 4)

Cheese Platter with Fresh Fruit

SUMMER BUFFET FOR TWELVE

Easy Antipasto Platter
(page 4)

Cheesy Walnut Flans
(Make double the recipe)
(page 8)

Polenta, Cheese and Prosciutto Loaf
(Make 2 loaves)
(page 16)

Mediterranean Fish Stew
(page 11)

Stuffed Cold Breast of Veal
(page 64)

Salad Supremo
(Make double the recipe)
(page 68)

Fennel and Orange Salad
(Make double the recipe)
(page 67)

Strawberries in Balsamic Vinegar
(Make double the recipe)
(page 75)

Cassata Siciliana
(page 81)

COUNTDOWN FOR SUMMER BUFFET

Use this countdown to ensure that both you and your guests can enjoy your Summer Buffet.

ONE WEEK BEFORE
✧ Prepare Marinated Olives for the Antipasto Platter.

TWO DAYS BEFORE
✧ Make Cassata Siciliana.

THE DAY BEFORE
✧ Assemble and cook Stuffed Cold Breast of Veal.
✧ Make Polenta, Cheese and Prosciutto Loaf.
✧ Make dressings for the Salad Supremo and the Fennel and Orange Salad.
✧ Make Creamy Tuna Spread for the Antipasto Platter.
✧ Make Vegetable Toss for the Antipasto Platter.
✧ Make Cheesy Walnut Flans.

THREE HOURS BEFORE SERVING
✧ Assemble Antipasto Platter.
✧ Assemble Fennel and Orange Salad, but do not dress.
✧ Assemble Salad Supremo, but do not dress.
✧ Prepare Strawberries in Balsamic Vinegar, cover and refrigerate.
✧ Make Crostini for the Antipasto Platter.
✧ Prepare Prosciutto with Melon Wedges for Antipasto Platter.
✧ Prepare ingredients for Mediterranean Fish Stew and make the sauce, but do not bring it to the boil.

ONE HOUR BEFORE SERVING
✧ Slice Stuffed Cold Breast of Veal.
✧ Slice Polenta, Cheese and Prosciutto Loaf.

JUST PRIOR TO SERVING
✧ Place Cheesy Walnut Flans in oven at 150°C (300°F/Gas 2) to heat for 10 minutes.
✧ Bring the sauce for the Mediterranean Fish Stew to the boil and complete cooking.
✧ Dress Fennel and Orange Salad. Dress Salad Supremo.

PERFECT ENTERTAINING

Entertaining is lots of fun, but for some it turns into an organisational nightmare of trying to get everything cooked at the right time and to the table hot. Following these tips will ensure that you have a perfect party every time.

Plan menus

Set aside some time to plan your party, if possible do this one to two weeks ahead of the intended date. Writing down your menu allows you to see quickly if you are going to serve two very similar dishes or use the same ingredients. Check the cooking methods you will be using to ensure that you include a variety. Menu planning eliminates the anxious feelings of 'Have I got enough food?' or 'Is the variety of food interesting?'

How to plan a menu

Planning a menu can be tackled in a number of ways. If you have absolutely no idea what you wish to serve, decide on the main course – it will get you going. After you have made that decision go on and plan the starter and dessert, remembering to select dishes that will complement the main course: a starter heavily flavoured with garlic will completely ruin the delicate taste of fish as a main course; with a heavy or rich main course, such as lasagne or a pork dish, the starter and dessert should be light; whereas a light main course, such as chicken or fish, allows for a richer dessert or starter. Desserts are the chance for the cook to show off great culinary skills, but remember that a rich dessert will not be appreciated if the first two courses have used lots of cream, eggs or butter.

The three most important things to remember when planning a meal are taste, colour and texture. Consider carefully how many things need to be prepared or cooked at the last minute. Preparing as much as possible in advance means that it will be easier to get all your food to the table at the right time. If you have a main course and two accompaniments that require last-minute attention you are either going to have to have someone to help you or one of the dishes is going to suffer. However, choosing as an accompaniment a salad or a dish that will happily sit for 30 minutes, will overcome this problem and will allow you the time you need to make the main dish absolutely perfect.

Timing is also an important consideration, starters that rely on perfect timing can be tricky as you must be sure that all your guests are going to arrive on time.

Shopping lists

Once you have decided on your menu, draw up a master grocery list. Shopping lists ensure that you don't forget vital ingredients and that you buy the correct quantities. When entertaining, divide the shopping list into those ingredients that are nonperishable and can therefore be purchased a week or more in advance, and those that have to be purchased the day before or on the day. With this sort of shopping list your shopping will not take as long on the day of your party and will give you more time to spend preparing and relaxing before your guests arrive.

Read recipes

If you are making a recipe for the first time, read through several times, as this will alert you to any special preparation requirements, such as soaking beans, marinating or making stock. You will also be advised of any unfamiliar techniques that can slow down the preparation and cooking time. Reading the recipe through and assembling all your ingredients before you start cooking will save you time. When entertaining, if you are trying out a new dish it is a good idea to have a practice run so that you are familiar with the recipe, when it really matters and there are no unpleasant surprises. This is particularly useful if the dish has techniques with which you are unfamiliar.

ITALIAN WINES

The climate and soil of Italy are perfect for wine production and every region produces wine. In fact Italy produces more wine than any other country in the world.

Aperitifs

Campari: This is a strong alcohol which is usually served with soda water.

Vermouth: A fortified wine. The French also have a vermouth but you will find that the Italian one is much sweeter.

White Wines

Frascati: Ideal for serving with fish and chicken. It is a light, dry straw-coloured wine which ranges from dry to sweet. The sweet frascati is known as Canellino and makes a good accompaniment to beans and gnocchi. Dry frascati is the best known of this group of wines.

Verdicchio: A young, light, fresh, fruity semi-dry wine.

Red Wines

Lambrusco: A light, dry, slightly sparkling wine, good to serve with meat meals.

Barbera: This robust red wine complements the full flavour of Italian food.

Chianti

Available as either red or white wine. As a young wine chianti is wonderfully fragrant and fruity; as it ages it becomes even better. This is the wine that is found in the straw-covered bottles so often associated with Italy.

Dessert Wines

Marsala: This fortifed full-flavoured sweet wine is named after a town on the island of Sicily. It is used mainly for cooking and dessert, however some varieties are also drunk as aperitifs.

Vin Santo: A dessert wine from Tuscany. It is made from grapes that are dried in the shade for several months. They are then pressed and the wine aged for four to five years in small oak casks. The casks are stored under the roof, thereby exposing the wine to variations in temperature, which adds to the unique flavour.

Sparkling Wines

Asti Spumanti: The best known sweet Italian sparkling wine that makes a perfect finish to a meal. It is made in vast quantities and exported all over the world.

Liqueurs

Galliano: A rich yellow liqueur flavoured with herbs.

Sambuca: A clear anise flavoured liqueur.

Amaretto: A rich toffee-coloured liqueur that tastes of almonds.

Frangelico: A delicious liqueur made from hazelnuts, berries, almonds, orange flowers and cinnamon.

DID YOU KNOW?

Wine production in some areas of Italy has been traced back to the Bronze and Iron Ages. It is believed that shepherds cultivated wild plants to produce wine.

❖

LEMON LIQUEUR

In Italy liqueurs are frequently made at home. The following liqueur used to be made by nearly everyone in southern Italy and was offered to visitors. In Italy it is called Liquore al limone. It is easy to make, so why not finish your next Italian dinner party with a glass.

Makes 1.2 litres (2 pt)

- ☐ **4 thick-skinned lemons**
- ☐ **750 mL (12 fl oz) vodka**
- ☐ **250 g (8 oz) sugar**
- ☐ **500 mL (8 fl oz) water**

1　Place lemons in a bowl of cold water and set aside to soak for 1 hour. Remove from water and dry with absorbent kitchen paper. Using a vegetable peeler carefully peel the rind from the lemons, taking care no white pith remains on the rind.

2　Place lemon rind in a wide-mouthed jar, pour over 500 mL (16 fl oz) of vodka, seal and set aside in a dark place for 3 days.

3　Combine sugar and water, bring to the boil and stir to dissolve sugar. Remove from heat, cover and set aside to cool for 2 hours.

4　Add the sugar mixture to the lemon rind mixture, strain through a paper coffee filter then place in a clean bottle. Return lemon rind to bottle and add remaining vodka. Seal and set aside in a dark place for 2 days.

5　Filter the liqueur through a paper coffee filter into a clean bottle, seal and set aside in a dark place for 7 days before using.

THE ITALIAN DELI

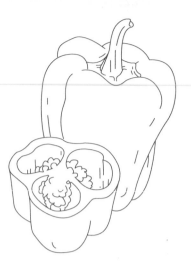

The basic ingredients for creating wonderful Italian meals are readily available. There are a number of convenience foods today, which save you some of the more time-consuming preparation steps. Don't scorn these – Italians use them all the time!

A good Italian grocer's shop or delicatessen will provide all the fundamental ingredients you will need for Italian cooking. Browsing along the shelves is an education and joy in itself, as Italian food must surely have the most attractive packaging in the world. Whether it's a box of biscuits with an 18th century label, or legs of proscuitto crudo in their own natural packaging hanging overhead, the food always looks interesting and inviting.

Here is a list of goods commonly found in the Italian deli with labelling or origins that may have stumped you in the past. For an explanation of olives, olive oils, pasta and cheeses, refer to the appropriate chapters.

Amaretti: These are almond flavoured crisp macaroons. They keep well stored in an airtight container.

Anchovies (acciughe): Fillets preserved in salt or oil. Italian anchovies are generally milder than those from other countries. Also anchovy paste.

Arborio rice: This is the rice from the Po Valley which has the special qualities for making risotto. The word 'superfino' sometimes appears on the label. If unavailable, look for vialone rice.

Ariosto: A mixture of herbs and spices for roast meats, in little sachets. No Italian housewife would be without a supply!

Baccala: This is dried salted cod and requires lengthy softening in cold water before cooking.

Balsamic vinegar (aceto balsamico): This syrupy and luscious vinegar from Modena is aged in wood to become thick and syrupy. It should be used sparingly.

Biscotti di prato: Hard biscuits with whole almonds; also known as cantucci or cantuccini. They are usually dunked in coffee or wine.

Bocconcini: Literally means a choice morsel. When applied to cheese it means small balls of fresh mozzarella.

Bresaola: Dried, cured beef fillet. It is served sliced thinly with oil and lemon juice.

Butter (burro): Butter in Italy is always unsalted.

Cannoli: These fried pastry cylinders have a sweet filling. They can be bought either filled or unfilled.

Capers (capperi): These are available either preserved in vinegar or salt. If preserved in salt they must be rinsed before using. The smaller the caper the better.

Carciofi (artichokes): Artichokes are available preserved in brine, oil or olive oil.

Carciofini: This refers to small artichokes or artichoke hearts.

Cedro: The glazed citron melon, used in dessert cooking or served in thin slices with cheese.

Cenci: These are fried pastries in the shape of knots or bows. They are usually served dusted with icing sugar.

Cetrioli: This refers to either gherkins or small cucumbers.

Coppa: Salted and dried pork sausage.

Cotechino: Large fresh, lightly spiced pork sausages.

Crostini: Pre-packaged, croutons for soup.

Dried tomatoes (pomodori secchi): These sun-dried tomatoes are usually marinated in oil, herbs and spices. The best are preserved in Extra Virgin Olive Oil. Sun-dried tomatoes vary in colour from bright, plump pieces to drier, darker ones. The darker drier ones have a more concentrated flavour.

Flour (farina): The flour used for pasta-making is semolina di grano duro or semola di grano duro on imported packets. If buying in bulk or the local product look for durum wheat flour.

Focaccia: Large flatbread, sprinkled with salt and oil then baked.

Lardo: Refined pork fat with a neutral flavour. It is used for roasts and some cakes and pastries. It is also known as strutto.

Mortadella: Cured pork sausage from Bologna. It is flavoured with white wine and spices, and usually black peppercorns and coriander.

Mustard fruits (mostarda di Cremona): Preserved mixed fruits in a sweet mustard syrup usually eaten with boiled meats.

Olive paste (pate di olive or polpa d'oliva): Made from both black and green olives. It is used on pasta, as a dip and to flavour sauces.

Pancetta: Unsmoked pork belly, cured in salt and spices. It is used to flavour cooked dishes.

Panettone: Spiced yeast cake with sultanas traditionally served at Christmas.

Peperoni: This name refers to sweet peppers, capsicums or pimientos. Can be roasted, marinated, stuffed or fried. Peperoncino are hot chilli peppers.

Polenta: Maize flour or cornmeal, usually yellow but a fine white meal is sometimes available. It can be coarse or fine grained and is sometimes labelled farina gialla or granoturco.

Porcini: Italian cepes or boletus mushrooms, sold dried in small packets, or in bulk. They need to be soaked in hot water for 20-30 minutes before using.

Prosciutto: Unsmoked, uncooked salted and air-cured ham, sold on the bone or boned. Serve thinly sliced or use in cooked dishes.

Rice (Ris, risi or riso): Also see Arborio.

Salame: This is the generic name for all cured sausages.

Saffron (zafferano): This is the dried stamens of the crocus flower. It is sold in the form of dried whole threads, or powdered.

Salume: Salt pork.

Salumi: Salted meat.

Salumeria: Delicatessen

Savoiardi: These are the wonderful sponge biscuits also known as ladyfingers.

Siena cake (panforte di siena): A rich, spicy flat cake with candied fruit and nuts.

Speck: Smoke-cured ham, with herbs and spices.

Torrone: Nougat.

Tomatoes (pomodori): Tomatoes are sold peeled and canned.

Tomato paste (concentrato di pomodoro): Tomato paste is available in double strength (doppio), or triple strength (triplo).

Triplo concentrato di pomodoro: Refers to Italian canned tomato products in general, they are superior to most others, the juice in a can of pomodori pelati is rich and thick and can be saved for a later use.

Vinegar (aceto): Wine-based vinegars are always used in Italian cooking.

Yeast (lievito): Little sachets of a special baking powder, which is packaged for a specific use. It is also known as lievito, for example lievito del pizzaiolo for pizza and savoury tarts, or the most well known, lievito vaniglinato for cakes and sweet baking.

THE ITALIAN PANTRY CHECKLIST

While Italian cooking uses many of the ingredients that you already have in your pantry there are a few ingredients that will give your Italian meals a more authentic flavour. This pantry checklist will help decide which items to have as staple and those that are useful to have in store for those times when you just must have Veal Marsala.

OILS AND VINEGARS
- ☐ olive oil
- ☐ extra virgin olive oil
- ☐ balsamic vinegar
- ☐ red wine vinegar
- ☐ white wine vinegar

RICE, PASTA, GRAINS, LEGUMES
- ☐ Arborio rice
- ☐ chick peas
- ☐ selection dried pulses
- ☐ selection canned pulses
- ☐ selection pasta shapes
- ☐ coloured pasta
- ☐ instant lasagne sheets

REFRIGERATOR ITEMS
- ☐ butter
- ☐ capers
- ☐ cream
- ☐ Gruyere or Emmenthal cheese
- ☐ Gorgonzola cheese
- ☐ mozzarella cheese
- ☐ fresh Parmesan cheese
- ☐ ricotta cheese
- ☐ selection olives
- ☐ marinated olives
- ☐ pesto
- ☐ sun-dried tomatoes
- ☐ yeast, fresh

CANNED FOODS
- ☐ canned anchovies
- ☐ canned artichoke hearts
- ☐ canned whole chestnuts
- ☐ canned Italian tomatoes
- ☐ canned concentrated tomato paste
- ☐ canned truffles

STORE CUPBOARD ITEMS
- ☐ amaretti
- ☐ chestnut puree
- ☐ grissini
- ☐ dried porcini mushrooms
- ☐ panettone
- ☐ pine nuts
- ☐ prepared sauce bases
- ☐ yeast, dried

MEAT AND POULTRY
(It is useful to keep a few of the fresh meat and poultry cuts in the freezer)
- ☐ chicken breast fillets
- ☐ rabbit
- ☐ veal cuts
- ☐ quail
- ☐ spatchcock
- ☐ mortadella
- ☐ prosciutto
- ☐ coppa
- ☐ salami

DRIED HERBS AND SPICES
- ☐ bayleaves
- ☐ marjoram
- ☐ oregano
- ☐ thyme
- ☐ sage
- ☐ dried chillies
- ☐ whole nutmeg
- ☐ fennel seeds
- ☐ cloves
- ☐ cinnamon
- ☐ black peppercorns
- ☐ selection dried fruit
- ☐ vanilla sugar
- ☐ saffron, strands and powder

ALCOHOL
- ☐ Marsala
- ☐ red wine
- ☐ white wine

FRESH PRODUCE
- ☐ eggplant (aubergine)
- ☐ fennel
- ☐ onions
- ☐ peppers
- ☐ witloof (chicory)
- ☐ zucchini
- ☐ fresh fruit
- ☐ garlic
- ☐ basil
- ☐ mint
- ☐ parsley
- ☐ tarragon

FREEZER FOODS
- ☐ selection meats
- ☐ frozen spinach
- ☐ frozen peas

GLOSSARY

Arborio rice	The classic risotto rice from Pedimont. If it is unavailable use any good quality risotto rice.
Balsamic vinegar	A vinegar from Modena aged in wood to become syrupy and luscious
Baste	To moisten meat or vegetables during cooking
Blanch	Drop food into a pan of boiling water. Return to the boil, then drain immediately and refresh under cold running water to stop the cooking and to retain the colour.
Blending	Mixing a liquid such as water with a dry ingredient such as cornflour. The mixture should be smooth, lump free and well combined.
Boil	Heating a liquid until the surface is bubbling all over
Bicarbonate of soda	Baking soda
Bocconcini cheese	Small balls of fresh mozzarella cheese. If it is unavailable use fresh mozzarella cut into cubes.
Breadcrumbs, dried	Use commercially packaged breadcrumbs
Breadcrumbs, fresh	1- or 2-day old bread made into crumbs
Cabbage	Savoy, common garden variety
Cheese, tasty	A firm good-tasting cheddar cheese
Chilli sauce	A sauce which includes chillies, salt and vinegar
Cornflour	Cornstarch, substitute arrowroot
Folding in	Combine ingredients quickly and gently, without deflating what is usually a light mixture. A large metal spoon is ideal for doing this.
Green, red or yellow peppers	Green, red or yellow capsicums
Gorgonzola cheese	If unavailable use any soft blue cheese, or blend some cream with a sharper, crumbly blue-vein in its place.
Knead	This is usually done on a lightly floured surface, the hands or fingertips are used to turn the outside edge of a mixture into the centre. Do this to either shape a mixture into a ball (pastry) or alter the nature of the mixture by working it with your hands (bread dough).
Plum tomatoes	Italian or egg tomatoes
Polenta	Cornmeal
Segment	Cut the peel and all white pith from citrus fruit, then cut between membranes joining segments
Simmer	Heating a liquid until the surface has the odd bubble bursting through
Snapper	A warm water sea fish with a delicate white flesh. Substitute sea bream.
Sour cream	Commercially soured cream
Stock	Homemade gives best results. For convenience, substitute 1 stock cube for every 500 mL (16 fl oz) water.
Three bean mix	Canned mixed beans
Toasting nuts	Spread the nuts evenly on an oven tray. Bake at 180°C (350°F/Gas 4) for 5-8 minutes or until lightly browned.

DICTIONARY

When browsing through a book about Italian food or working through a menu or recipe, a term sometimes crops up which is unfamiliar or at best, unclear. This list of words and phrases commonly used around an Italian kitchen may help make your reading more enjoyable.

Affumicato	Smoked
Agio e ogio	Garlic and oil, as a dressing
Al dente	To the tooth, a texture with some bite to it
Al forno/alla fornaia	In the oven; baked or roasted
Antipasto	The very first course of a meal, starters
Arrosto	Roasted, baked
Asciutto	Dry, as in pasta asciutto
Bollito	Boiled, particularly boiled meat
Cacciatora	Hunter's style
Caldo	Hot
Casalinga	Homemade
Condito	Dressed, as in a salad
Contorno	Vegetable dish, garnish
Cotto	Cooked
Crudo	Raw, uncooked
Cucina	Kitchen
Diavola	Devilled, or with a spicy sauce
Dolce	Sweets, dessert
Farcito	Stuffed
Fritto misto	Mixed fry
Freddo	Cold
Fresco	Fresh, cool
Fritto	Fried
Grasso	Fat
Integrale	Wholemeal
Il primo	The meal course between antipasto and the main course, consisting of soup, pasta, risotto or polenta
Il secondo	The main course of a meal
Magro	Thin, lean
Paglia e fieno	Straw and hay, meaning green and white
Pelato	Peeled
Petto	Breast, for example breast of chicken
Piatto	Plate
Ragu	Rich meat sauce
Ripieno	Stuffed
Rotolo	Roll, as in a swiss roll
Rustico	Rustic
Saor	Soused, as with fish
Secco	Dry
Soffritto	A mixture of chopped vegetables fried in butter or oil used as a flavour base for soups, sauces and stews
Sugo	Sauce, usually for pasta
Tavola	Table
Tritato	Minced, finely chopped
Verde	Green

USEFUL INFORMATION

In this book, fresh ingredients are given in grams and the nearest equivalent in ounces and pounds so you know how much to buy. A small inexpensive set of kitchen scales is always handy and very easy to use. Other ingredients in our recipes are given in spoons, so you will need a set of measuring spoons (1 tablespoon, 1 teaspoon, 1/2 teaspoon and 1/4 teaspoon) and a transparent graduated measuring jug (1 litre or 250 mL) for measuring liquids. Spoon measures are level.

MEASURING UP

Metric Measuring Cups

60 mL	2 fl oz	1/4 cup
80 mL	2 1/2 fl oz	1/3 cup
125 mL	4 fl oz	1/2 cup
250 mL	8 fl oz	1 cup

Metric Measuring Spoons

1/4 teaspoon	1.25 mL
1/2 teaspoon	2.5 mL
1 teaspoon	5 mL
1 tablespoon	20 mL

OVEN TEMPERATURES

°C	°F	Gas Mark
120	250	1/2
140	275	1
150	300	2
160	325	3
180	350	4
190	375	5
200	400	6
220	425	7
240	475	8
250	500	9

MEASURING DRY INGREDIENTS

Metric	Imperial
15 g	1/2 oz
30 g	1 oz
60 g	2 oz
90 g	3 oz
125 g	4 oz
155 g	5 oz
185 g	6 oz
220 g	7 oz
250 g	8 oz
280 g	9 oz
315 g	10 oz
350 g	11 oz
375 g	12 oz
410 g	13 oz
440 g	14 oz
470 g	15 oz
500 g	16 oz (1 lb)
750 g	1 lb 8 oz
1 kg	2 lb
1.5 kg	3 lb
2 kg	4 lb
2.5 kg	5 lb

MEASURING LIQUIDS

Metric	Imperial	Cup
30 mL	1 fl oz	
60 mL	2 fl oz	1/4 cup
90 mL	3 fl oz	
125 mL	4 fl oz	1/2 cup
155 mL	5 fl oz	
170 mL	5 1/2 fl oz	2/3 cup
185 mL	6 fl oz	
220 mL	7 fl oz	
250 mL	8 fl oz	1 cup
500 mL	16 fl oz	2 cups
600 mL	20 fl oz (1 pt)	
750 mL	1 1/4 pt	
1 litre	1 3/4 pt	4 cups
1.2 litres	2 pt	
1.5 litres	2 1/2 pt	
1.8 litres	3 pt	
2 litres	3 1/2 pt	
2.5 litres	4 pt	

QUICK CONVERTER

Metric	Imperial
5 mm	1/4 in
1 cm	1/2 in
2 cm	3/4 in
2.5 cm	1 in
5 cm	2 in
10 cm	4 in
15 cm	6 in
20 cm	8 in
23 cm	9 in
25 cm	10 in
30 cm	12 in

INDEX

ACKNOWLEDGMENTS

The publishers wish to thank the following Admiral Appliances; Black & Decker (Australasia) Pty Ltd; Blanco Appliances; Knebel Kitchens; Leigh Mardon Pty Ltd; Master Foods of Australia; Meadow Lea Foods; Namco Cookware; Ricegrowers' Co-op Mills Ltd; Sunbeam Corporation Ltd; Tycraft Pty Ltd distributors of Braun, Australia; White Wings Foods for their assistance during recipe testing.

Passello for supplying all the pasta for this book.

Penny Cox for her assistance during recipe testing.

Donna Hay for her assistance during recipe testing and photography.

Cover props: *Platter* Jenny Orchard, *Background* Porters Lime Wash, *Tiles* Country Foors